CHICAGO PUBLIC LIBRARY
BUSINESS / SCIENCE / TECHNOLOGY
400 S. STATE ST.   60605

OCR →

D1507672

BUSINESS/SCIENCE/TECHNOLOGY DIVISION
CHICAGO PUBLIC LIBRARY
400 SOUTH STATE STREET
CHICAGO, IL 60605

CHICAGO PUBLIC LIBRARY

R03005 11737

Living and Loving with Asperger Syndrome

of related interest

An Asperger Marriage
Gisela and Christopher Slater-Walker
Foreword by Tony Attwood
ISBN 1 84310 017 7

Asperger Syndrome and Long-Term Relationships
Ashley Stanford
Foreword by Liane Holliday Willey
ISBN 1 84310 734 1

Aspergers in Love
Maxine Aston
ISBN 184310 1157

Freaks, Geeks and Asperger Syndrome
A User Guide to Adolescence
Luke Jackson
Foreword by Tony Attwood
ISBN 1 84310 098 3

Asperger's Syndrome
A Guide for Parents and Professionals
Tony Attwood
Foreword by Lorna Wing
ISBN 1 85302 577 1

Living and Loving with Asperger Syndrome

Family Viewpoints

Patrick, Estelle and Jared McCabe

RC 553 .A88 M376 2003
McCabe, Patrick, 1958-
Living and loving with
  Asperger syndrome

Jessica Kingsley Publishers
London and Philadelphia

All rights reserved. No part of this publication may be reproduced in any material form (including photocopying or storing it in any medium by electronic means and whether or not transiently or incidentally to some other use of this publication) without the written permission of the copyright owner except in accordance with the provisions of the Copyright, Designs and Patents Act 1988 or under the terms of a licence issued by the Copyright Licensing Agency Ltd, 90 Tottenham Court Road, London, England W1P 9HE. Applications for the copyright owner's written permission to reproduce any part of this publication should be addressed to the publisher.
Warning: The doing of an unauthorised act in relation to a copyright work may result in both a civil claim for damages and criminal prosecution.

The right of the contributors to be identified as authors of this work has been asserted by them in accordance with the Copyright, Designs and Patents Act 1988.

First published in the United Kingdom in 2003
by Jessica Kingsley Publishers Ltd
116 Pentonville Road
London N1 9JB, England
and
325 Chestnut Street
Philadelphia, PA 19106, USA

www.jkp.com

Copyright © 2003 Patrick, Estelle and Jared McCabe

Library of Congress Cataloging in Publication Data
A CIP catalog record for this book is available from the Library of Congress

British Library Cataloguing in Publication Data
A CIP catalogue record for this book is available from the British Library

ISBN 1 84310 744 9

Printed and Bound in Great Britain by
Athenaeum Press, Gateshead, Tyne and Wear

R03005 11737

BUSINESS/SCIENCE/TECHNOLOGY DIVISION
CHICAGO PUBLIC LIBRARY
400 SOUTH STATE STREET.
CHICAGO, IL 60605

Contents

Biographical Note

Having Asperger Syndrome for forty-four years makes Patrick well qualified to write on this topic. He has a varied background in the field of writing. Patrick has created manuals for his work with the Denver Rescue Mission and currently writes articles for organizational newsletters. While in university, he wrote a seven-chapter thesis. Patrick has taken college level composition courses as well as attending a nationally recognized writer's seminar.

Estelle has taught writing and has edited for ten years while home schooling her son Jared. Presently, she uses her writing skills in her position as the PASS Coordinator at the local junior high school in her hometown of Wellington, CO. (PASS is an acronym for Parallel Advocate Support System, a program which has been set up to help "at risk" students who need extra help with their schoolwork, as well as emotional support.)

Jared has developed his writing abilities during his school years. He has taken numerous writing courses through correspondence during this time period, graded by professional writers and editors. Now in college, he continues to hone his writing skills.

Acknowledgements

As a family, we'd like to thank our God, who loves all people equally. Clearly, He has created us all differently, but sees the value that each of us retain. We'd like to thank all of our friends who have encouraged us through life, through the writing of this book, including those who have been willing to be interviewed as part of it. Our lives are much richer because of you.

Introduction

What is this book about? It is a collaborative effort on the parts of my wife (Estelle), son (Jared), and myself (the one with Asperger Syndrome). We have included interviews with co-workers and friends. We consider this an effort to help other Asperger families do more than cope with having this Pervasive Developmental Disorder (PDD) in their families.

At the time of this writing Estelle is forty years old, Jared is seventeen, and I am forty-four. We have been married eighteen years. Estelle and I have always been committed to each other. We have always acknowledged that, and openly talked about our love for each other with each other. We have also had very hard times being married to each other. All three of us have had significant struggles in regards to Jared's upbringing.

You are probably thinking this is true for 98 percent of all couples and families! I am sure it is. One difference with us is that I have Asperger's Syndrome. Once we discovered what my "problem" was, we went to work as a family. We have learned what it has meant and means in our every day lives, our relationships at work and socially, and in our marriage. We have learned much and continue to learn more as we spend more time together. We hope to share some of what we have learned with you in a way that will help you and your family enjoy each other more, and influence you, your family, co-workers and friends in a positive direction.

1

A Bird's Eye View

A three-year-old boy sat on a wooden rooster in a park. He saw his family: mom, dad, and siblings standing nearby. He knew he was connected to them somehow. He was alone with them, all alone, even with them nearby. Not lonely or having a feeling of loneliness, he truly was simply, entirely alone.

As an adult I was looking at photographs with my mother. I saw the little boy on the rooster and the family next to him. I realized then it wasn't a dream or thought; I really had sat on the rooster in the park. My mother had explained to me, "You were different from the very beginning." I was told we were family. In fact, we really were blood relatives. The word *family* was my thread of connection to them.

For us Asperger people, words are of extreme importance. They are pictures, connections of understanding, peace, and direction. For me, not only does every word need to be exactly correct, so does my behavior, the order of the day, the order of my thinking, and others' behavior. People need to say what they mean and mean what they say. I cannot count the number of times people have said to me they would do something "in a couple of days." How many times has someone said to you, "I'll do it tomorrow?" Often times people exaggerate and say things like: "That car almost hit that kid," or "He looks like he got hit by a Mac truck."

These people have no idea how hard that is for some of us. I want to trust them and plan for their work to be done in "a couple of days." On the third day, I look for it so I can do my own work on the subject, or simply review theirs to return it corrected. I see the deadline on a calendar in my mind. They simply blew the project timeline up! I knew I would review it; they would have so many days to correct it and I could get it in to my boss two days ahead of time. Now, only God knows when they will get it done. I become energized; my arms come alive with feeling. I have to deal with this *right now*! Waiting will only cause the frustration to grow. "I'll do it tomorrow," means tomorrow, doesn't it? Of course it does. I want to plan my day. It is tomorrow. I call to ask what time I should come by to pick up the completed project. I hear stress in my co-worker's voice that is not normally there as he says, "I didn't mean that fast; I meant I'll do it after I've finished the project I'm on." I say "OK," and explain the importance of timeliness, as my whole body fires up. I hang up the phone, having lost trust in this person and wondering how could he have said, "I'll do it tomorrow," if he knew it would be two or three days away. My plans for the day must be changed. I hate that; my frustration level puts me on edge, ready to jump at something, or jerk back when touched.

When someone says, "That car almost hit that kid," I visualize a child in the street sitting down looking at a toy with his back to traffic. A car speeds by and barely misses the child by 1/16th of an inch. You cannot tell for a second or two if the child was hit or not. I am ready to go chase down the driver of the car to stop him. With all my senses on total alert, my body is one mass of energy and totally focused on getting this car found and stopped. We can't let someone else get hurt! Then, as I hear the details of the story, I find out the child was on the sidewalk, at least three feet from the car and the child was looking at the car the whole time and never tried to run away from the car. As I realize this, I want to yell, "Why did you say the kid almost got hit by the car? The car was at least three feet away!" Of course, my affect is very calm and unemotional through the whole ordeal. In fact, people comment on why I am not upset, or on how calm I remain through crisis.

Another type of word confusion is, "He looks like a truck ran over him." Once I've heard that, I have to find out what it means. Does he have a black eye, disheveled shirt, bags under his eyes, or what? I can't let go until I have a more accurate visual picture of what they mean by that cliché. When I ask someone where the crescent wrench is and he says, "over there," I want to scream. "Over there" is saying, start looking everywhere but here. I asked so I wouldn't have to look! Why not just say "on the bench," "near the grinder," etc.

An important element of all of this is that the stress and energized body does not go away quickly. In fact, it usually takes me hours to feel calm again, *if* nothing else happens. The majority of life is stress, period. Well, now you have an idea of the importance of communication in the life of a person with Asperger Syndrome. I hope these examples and explanations help you better understand your Asperger family member.

Let's look at structure, order, and language. The way we think is in order, as well as visually. I think of it as a filing system in my head. While attending a Spanish language school about three years ago, I discovered some important insights into my own mind. I noticed that after doing my workbook, listening to audiotapes and studying my other homework, I believed I was ready for class the next day. In fact, I was ready. But something strange was happening to me. After the first ten minutes in class, I was lost. This, of course, was frustrating. It was also embarrassing, as we had to recite and modify sentences out loud in Spanish in front of our peers. I didn't have any problem doing this at home with audiotapes, but I did in class. It was not typical peer pressure that affected me, though; it was something else.

The first exercise we did in class was to do recitation. The teacher would pick different students randomly as we worked through the exercises out loud. If I went first, I got the modification correct. If I went after anyone who made a mistake or said it differently than expected, I lost it. (Sometimes I would visualize, with my eyes open, an explosion like fireworks in the sky.) I could not follow the class after that; it was confusing as the students went on from one sentence to another. I could rarely get back on track. I was doing well in the classes where we did not have to go through this exercise. I also knew I had some intellectual ability.

After graduating twelfth from the bottom out of 743 kids in high school, I did well in college. I had an AGS degree with a 3.9 grade point average and a BS degree with a 4.0 grade point average. I had received one B from a teacher who informed us the first day of class that during his thirteen years of teaching he had never given a student an A for his class. He said no one had ever earned one from him. I received a C+ in Algebra, but As in the rest of my classes. I couldn't understand what was happening to me in the language school. I began seeing a psychologist with an educational testing background. Dr McCoy turned out to be a fine psychologist. Not only did he help me understand my learning process better, he helped Estelle and I understand each other better. Our marriage has been richer for it.

I learned that what had happened in some high school classes was happening again in the language school. Whenever the instruction got out of order, or was not what I had expected, I got lost and confused. In junior high school I gave up trying; I wasn't going to this time. I had learned by now that I wasn't stupid. In college I was given material to learn and papers to write or tests to take, many were essays or multiple choice. I excelled because I taught myself the material in an order my brain accepted. I did this for all classes except Algebra. There was that classroom exercise problem again! Even though I used a graduate student tutor prior to class, I would get lost within ten minutes after the exercises started.

Now, I will unfold some thoughts about behavior. Behavior needs to be in order, at least that is my perception of the Asperger mind. We have a need for consistency. This need seems to be universal in almost every area of life, in general ways. I have read about how Asperger people are drawn to occupations like education, engineering, etc., areas where their IQs can be used and yet they are allowed to work primarily on their own, in their way. I do think we are also drawn into structured occupations that sometimes involve interacting with people. I cannot say I recommend this; however, it has been true in my case.

As I reflect on my work history and what I have chosen, I see clearly that something inherently led me to structure. I believe that something was that I could not think of other occupations visually in an orderly way in my mind. I could not be a salesman. The thought of living off an unpredictable paycheck cannot be formed or visualized in my mind. I never understood what a professor really did because of my class time confusion. I never heard an explanation of an engineer that I could visualize, probably because I heard bits and pieces of the different types of engineers without an explanation. I have since learned to use dictionaries and encyclopedias to clarify murky perceptions of things I hear about. Often, people do not explain them in order, but the books usually do. Johannes Gutenberg's invention of the printing press is a true friend of the Asperger people.

At different times as a teenager, I dreamed about and visualized being a sailor, a police officer, and a green beret soldier. I realize now, all of those occupations required everyone to behave in a well-established manner that *everyone* knew about and understood. I saw images of them on TV and story lines in movies that explained their work. I turned eighteen in boot camp. The structure of the Navy was comforting. It was really clear that all of us were told the same rules on how to behave. This was understandable and wonderful to me. I finally had a sense of being on a level playing field with the others around me. Life was not subjective anymore. Life was organized with a clear view of what was supposed to happen. Social cues and reading messages between the lines in people's conversation was very insignificant compared to following orders and getting the job done!

I used the system to gain rank, and with it more pay. Clearly systems became friends of mine. Even if they were slow, they were the same for everyone. It didn't matter what club you were in or what sport you played or if you didn't. Teachers' pets, guidance counselors' favorites and class presidents had no meaning in the military. I did not have to be socially "in." All I had to do was follow the rules, work hard, and take tests. Man, this was what I was made for! On the flight deck of the aircraft carrier I was on, everyone wore a certain color of jersey and life vest that told everyone else what job they did. There was red, green, blue, yellow, brown, and purple. You could see at a glance who was doing what, my kind of world!

When my time was up in the Navy, I wanted a new challenge. Not realizing how much I enjoyed or needed the structure, I tried working with crop dusters for a while. I quickly started to pursue structure again, in the form of a police department. Nine months out of the Navy, I started working as a police officer in California. The structure was great. I had the rank structure of the department *and* I had city ordinances, a state vehicle code and a state penal code that told me how everyone was supposed to behave. This was right up my alley. I was just beginning to see a strong need for structure in life.

As seems to be typical with Asperger people, I needed a new challenge after nearly two years on the force. I decided to switch to another structured environment, although I did not look at it that way. I was driven by the need for a challenge and recognized a desire for structure. I did not like the push and pull to control me that it had on my life, yet I was seeing it's reality. I pursued my third visualized occupation.

I joined the Army with a contract for Airborne, Special Forces, and Military Intelligence. I also met my future bride during this time. I never became a Green Beret, but I did hold a top secret clearance and I did work in Intelligence. By now, I saw my need for structure and a college education. I took some college classes while a police officer and continued it off and on while in the Army. After four years in the Army, I was prepared to make the military a career. Then I was told I would have to go to Turkey without my wife and two-and-a-half-year-old son for a year.

I was torn between my loyalty to them and my desire for an honorable career. I have read that Asperger people are unusually loyal. I sense an intense loyalty to those that I am committed to. I chose to be with my young son Jared and my wife Estelle. I couldn't imagine (literally) leaving my little boy without a dad for a year because of a career that *I* wanted. I left the military and ended up working as a police officer for the Veteran's Administration. Imagine that! Asperger Syndrome had hugely influenced my life in so many ways and yet I didn't have a name for it, or even know that I had a "disorder."

I finished an Associate's degree. I wasn't making enough money to really support my family. I tried the private sector for work again and at the four-month mark I found myself working for the Department of Justice. I just had to have the structure, and was really beginning to accept that. I knew I would have a set work schedule and a certain amount of pay. I started as a correctional officer and continued college. Three months after receiving my Bachelor's degree, I was selected for a promotion to case manager and transferred to another prison complex in Texas.

After some time I was driven for more challenge. As Estelle puts it, "Once you conquer something, you are done with it." I was driven on to a position as a partially supported missionary in a relatively structured environment. After about two-and-a-half years, I was promoted to the administration level. In that position for a little more than a year, I needed another challenge. Since we were in a Spanish speaking country and I realized how poor my

Spanish grammar was, we became fully supported missionaries and went to language school.

I had developed enough faith in God through the structure He provided and experience with Him to do it. That structure came through prayer letters, presentations, and of, course, very clear-cut promises from Him in the Bible. I had shifted my structure from agencies, to God. This happened after experiencing bouts of hepatitis, typhoid and little money at times. He proved to be faithful and He kept His part of the commitment.

After our time at language school we were asked to work at our ministry's headquarters. I could not compute just learning Spanish better and moving to Indiana. It wouldn't fit into my brain's filing system. I had no category to file it under. We moved to Colorado where we knew there was an abundance of Spanish speaking migrant workers. In my structured thinking, I found the line of ordered thinking; I had to use what I had just learned.

Currently, I am working as the Operations and Facilities Manager for a rescue mission, a 100-acre farm with 60 homeless men living on it. As you can guess, it is a structured environment. Everybody operates under the guidelines of a handbook. Even as I write this I see even more so how the need for structure and challenge have had such a grip on me. Realizing the powerful pulls of challenge and structure, Asperger people can better plan and order their futures. This knowledge is helpful to all of us in choosing a career and life direction.

Well, now you have a bird's eye view of how at least one Asperger person sees the world. I've articulated the need for correct words, correct behavior for others and myself, the need for ordered thoughts, and the powerful pull for challenge and structure in our lives. The next chapter will explain how all this is played out in day-to-day married life. Estelle has some very interesting words for you in this next chapter. She is a wonderful wife and continues to teach me how to laugh through our struggles.

2

Living with an Asperger Husband

The year was 1983. A casual setting, he was dressed formally. Wearing a buttoned up lime green polyester sixties suit, he had a white long sleeved dress shirt but no tie. On his feet were brown suede shoes. The suit was too small for his twenty-four-year-old athletic body. The sleeves were too short. The jacket was too tight. The pant hems fell just to his ankles revealing black cotton socks. The shoes had long ago been worn down to the soles, leaving him walking on the sides of his feet. Though it looked like he walked out of the local Salvation Army, in reality, he was wearing one of his two favorite suits from years past. Amazing. Even more amazing was the confidence that exuded from him.

The women sought after him at the weekly Bible study meetings we both attended. The men respected him for his leadership, and wisdom. I often watched him meeting the needs of those around him with compassion and concern. Needless to say, I fell for him. That was almost nineteen years ago.

Our first years of marriage were met with only normal conflicts, or so I thought. The smallest differences between us brought strife and extreme frustration. But wasn't that what all newly married couples went through? Patrick and I just needed to get to know each other better. And being "in love" helped us overlook the confusion.

As time went on our differences grew, as well as the confusion. Was it me? My actions seemed to cause great amounts of stress. Inappropriate word usage, using generalization in a conversation, saying something flippantly without thinking, not having "edible" food in the house, or being late, could easily send him into a frenzied state. Trying to understand me stressed him into a state of immobilization. He would lie down, and cover his eyes, while remaining completely still and quiet. What happened? I didn't understand.

Trying to figure out why we had such conflict led us to seek the advice of a counselor. This stress was hurting our marriage and building a wall of separation. To me, the issues were insignificant. Why was Patrick making such a big deal about things? To Patrick, these were life-stopping issues. How could I not see what I was doing to him? Did I not respect him enough to change my stress-creating behavior? We discussed our IQ differences. Could that be the problem? I was convinced that Patrick's IQ was way beyond normal. He did not think on the average level, but on things out of my range. He enjoyed discussing deep philosophical issues, yet when I tried to engage him in "regular conversation," more conflict ensued. He made the simple things of life complex and the most complicated simple.

Our new focus of seeing each other as individuals with varied backgrounds, as advised by the counselor, only gave us some breathing room. But in time, the stress returned in full force. Initially, I blamed myself. I felt that no matter how hard I tried there was no peace to be found. I stuffed the anger year after year. When I could no longer hold it in, I began to resent Patrick. Believing he was making big issues out of nothing made me quite angry. He would *freak* over something little, then blame me for it! I eventually decided it was his problem. He would have to get over it.

Several things happened to bring about a turning point in our lives. I finally started listening to Patrick. I began to see the stress that Jared was feeling due to the conflict in our lives. And, I also began to realistically look at issues in my own life I needed to deal with.

For many years Patrick had been trying to "teach me" how to peacefully live with him, but I would not listen. His explanations did not make any sense to me. I also did not want to stop and change. I believed that most of our conflict was due to his being too picky and demanding to have things his way.

Jared entered puberty and Mom and Dad were no longer perfect. Our normal teenager, being very intelligent, somehow discovered that things weren't quite right. Before Patrick's Asperger diagnosis, I tried to find every possible explanation for his *different* behavior. But, that no longer worked. Dad's Dr Jeckyl and Mr Hyde performances did not continue unnoticed. Jared finally said to me, "No, Mom, something is definitely wrong with Dad. That just isn't like him. He is like two different people." Jared's statement helped jolt me into reality. I did not want to believe that Patrick and I had some major problems. But seeing that Jared was being affected by our problem, I could no longer be in denial. Patrick and I could struggle, but our son should not have to suffer. Again Patrick and I sought help.

Getting an Asperger diagnosis gave our family direction. It gave us the freedom to move forward. I began to see Patrick differently. He would focus in on minute, trivial issues. He would explode, then go on and on and on about whatever was bothering him. I stopped to notice his frustration for what it was instead of being angry with him for being frustrated. I still couldn't seem to see any pattern to what would set him off. I did notice that when I would be calm and tried to understand, he became calm. But when I reacted emotionally, it was like igniting a bomb! He also felt terrible when he treated me badly. I began to realize that he was just as bothered by his outbursts as I was. This was very helpful to me.

For a teenager, having "something different about Dad" is not easy to accept. Focusing on the fact that everyone has differences, and accepting others regardless of those differences have been our focal points. However, Jared is quite normal and likes to see his parents' reactions to his various behaviors. He is quickly realizing that he may secure two quite varied responses. When Jared pushes Dr Jeckyl's buttons, he may face lifelong grounding, while

Mr Hyde may just laugh at his attempts to annoy him. He has learned to check out whom he is dealing with *before* testing his limits.

Jared is still learning that regular doses of honest communication with Dad will keep him out of trouble. He has also come to realize that negative attitudes are *felt* and body language is read by his dad a long distance away. Mom's job as an interpreter and an encourager sure does come in handy when he's in trouble. Jared is smart to secure a "reality check" from me at those times. He also asks my intervention or advice on how to negotiate with Dad. However, simple, honest communication with Dad is the key to a quick resolution, which is what we all want.

When I look back, I am ashamed of my careless responses and lack of compassion in dealing with Patrick. If I had listened to him earlier and made simple changes we could have avoided much heartache in our relationship. As I now realize the challenges Patrick faces daily I more deeply appreciate him. He has adapted significantly in life and the effort he puts into our relationship to make me happy puts me to shame. I am truly loved.

Patrick has so many positive qualities which he uses to love others. He is extremely sensitive and loving. Knowing how criticism and misunderstanding feels, he always works to build others up. Patrick notices the underdog and goes to bat for him. He is generous with his compliments, gifts, time and attention. He is a loyal and committed family man. Patrick is concerned about the good of our family and works hard to protect it. Friends and co-workers notice how spoiled I am by Patrick's thoughtfulness and chivalry. I am cared for and nurtured beyond my expectations.

Some of Patrick's differences are now enjoyable to me or even quite funny. My husband *likes* sleeping on the couch occasionally, but not because he's in trouble. It is one way for him to be alone and to truly unwind. Sometimes when he doesn't feel smothered he will invite me to sleep on the couch with him! I now make a game of Patrick's "rejection" of my romantic attempts. I warn him ahead of time that I am going to hug him or show him affection. I tell him he shouldn't tell his wife not to hurt him when I just want to cuddle. Imagine having to ask your husband of eighteen years for a hug! Or being told your kisses feel like a drill putting a hole in his cheek! Patrick also enjoys listening to Morse code, as it is soothing to his ears. He will play it as one puts on a good CD to relax to. Patrick enjoys a good chat in the wee hours of the morning. Sometimes I will hear a friendly voice at 4am inviting me out into the living room to talk. Patrick is very tender with animals. He enters their world and can see from their perspective, becoming an advocate for them. Often he will ask me to do or change something for our pets in a way that I know he can feel what they are feeling.

Patrick regularly seeks out my help in understanding how to live peacefully in this "world of humanoids." We have made several changes to help him to "blend in" a little better. We replaced a ten year old hairstyle with a more modern one. I've convinced him to throw out some of his favorite T-shirts that you could see through. The

Salvation Army has acquired many of his outgrown or out of style pants. And the shoes we've simply thrown away!

Patrick still has a "uniform" to pick from each day; however, now his clothes are modern and match well – except for the days when he feels especially eccentric. On those days he may match painted jeans with a nice dress shirt or dress pants with tennis shoes. I really try hard not to be upset with him. He has told me that I can have almost anything I want from him if I will simply ask. So if it's important for me to have him wear certain clothes on a special occasion, I surely better ask before he dresses because once he's dressed, he's dressed. And I might really be in for a surprise!

I have learned many other ways in which I can help keep Patrick's highly sensitized sensory system from going into overload. Using correct language, a pleasant tone of voice and non-threatening body language helps him to be calm. My calmness is a balm to him. My "freaking out" sends shock waves through his body taking sometimes days to get over. Answering questions exactly the way presented decreases his stress level. A "yes" or "no" is more than sufficient most times. When I allow him to sit without being distracted, he can desensitize. My answering the phone or dealing with people keeps him from overstimulating his sensory system. Living by systems or rules we have set up in our home gives him structure he can count on. We have clearly defined areas of responsibilities making home a place of peace.

Patrick is teachable. When he can ask my perception of others' behavior, he learns to understand them, thus allowing continued relationships. I also can interpret him for others when the need arises. Patrick needs the freedom to be himself so I don't try to make him into what I think he should be. Since Patrick deeply cares for Jared and me, I need to allow him to love us the way he wants to. I need to be honest with him at all times so he can trust me. He doesn't want to be the focus or have us catering to his needs. When I have food he can eat available, he can take care of himself, which keeps him from feeling dependent on me. When I make home life consistent and mellow, he can use his energy to give us what we need.

An area of life that has caused extreme frustration for both of us has been food. Never did I think that food would become such an issue. At one point I tried to quit my "job" as a cook, but my resignation was not accepted! "What's to eat?" became the question I most dreaded.

Needing sameness makes cooking a bore and a chore. Meals can be quite boring when you can't mix one item with another. For my husband, every item must be plain and separated on the plate. And relaxing on the job has resulted in inedible food. If the food cooks too long, the consistency is affected. Or if I am thinking about something when the salt gets added, the taste will be different, creating such a shock that Patrick cannot eat it when he tries. Meals also need to be eaten at the same time each day. Not being able to eat "on time" will throw Patrick's whole day off. Meals are a constant he needs to count on.

Another interesting factor that took me forever to comprehend was the dessert issue. While waiting for dinner, Patrick would eat the last few cookies or other sweet I had available. After enjoying our meal, he'd ask, "What's for dessert?" I'd go looking for the cookies only to find that he had eaten them. Even though he had had his sweets, it wasn't "dessert" since it was eaten *before* dinner, not *after*!

Social life has been a real issue in the past! Patrick and I have since worked out a pretty good plan that seems to work well for us. Before, dinners and other get-togethers presented a problem. Many times events were scheduled and looked forward to by Jared and myself, then cancelled at the last moment. Patrick had had just too much people exposure and needed a break. He either didn't feel well or was irritable and knew he was not in the mood to deal with people.

Although we want and need to spend time with others, we have to make modifications to keep Patrick's world in order. If we are going to a dinner, I inconspicuously find out in advance what will be served to allow Patrick to eat ahead of time, if he can't eat the food to be served. We have certain routines set up so I can "rescue" him from conversations he can't get out of, or help him to leave from work when he needs to. Planning ahead to leave early from a function allows Patrick to avoid long drawn out good-byes and gives Patrick the freedom to complete his evening routine. We avoid last minute social events so Patrick can have the time he needs to prepare for social time. He takes ample people breaks beforehand so he can be nice to us "humanoids." It also keeps him from being irritable because of over-stimulation, doing

Asperger tics (e.g. raising his eyebrows, pulling on his beard and stretching his lips repeatedly), or having to cancel out at the last moment.

Although Patrick is stressed by too much time with people, one of his special interests is people, a rarity I think, due to the anti-social nature of Asperger folks. The study of people is a hobby for him. Many times we've gone to the mall to eat a cookie and watch people. Many of our conversations are filled with the whys and hows of people. Patrick has such a deep love for the people around him. He continually seeks to love them by giving and sharing.

Our family truly has benefited from acknowledging the label of Asperger Syndrome. It has opened our eyes to reveal a world of very talented and gifted people to whom the world owes much. Having been touched by the life of one of them has made me a better person. Looking through Patrick's eyes is helping me to appreciate much in life that I have taken for granted. I look forward to what richness we will enjoy as we uncover more of the hidden secrets of Asperger Syndrome.

3

Staying Married and Enjoying it!

To keep a marriage healthy and enjoy one's spouse requires a great deal of effort. However, adding an extra element of Asperger Syndrome to the equation causes this effort to become much greater. In this chapter, Patrick and I will separately discuss some of the more stressful issues we face in our daily lives and how we have learned to deal with them. We will cover intimacy, socialization, clothing, routines, communication, time alone and trust.

A word from Estelle...

An Asperger person vitally needs touch! However, mental preparation has to be made for this type of stimulation to be a positive experience for an Asperger person. Touch can be calming or shocking, depending on how and when it is performed. The feeling of skin to skin can go unfelt if the receiving person is not properly prepared. At other times this sensation can have such a negative effect that the Asperger person will recoil, as if in pain. I learned this the hard way.

Throughout our many years of marriage I have lovingly hugged Patrick or kissed him on the cheek. Frequently this action generated a negative response, a recoiled stiffened body, with a stoic face. At first, being the cheerful optimist, I did not even notice. Gradually, I finally realized what was happening and my feelings were hurt. Patrick acted like he loved me, so why was he behaving in this manner? He responded that he "just needed to get ready for it." That didn't make sense! How does anyone have to prepare to receive love? Eventually I decided to make a game of it. I warned him before kissing him so he could have the time he needed to connect my love with the action. That helped both of us considerably. However, as the years went by, the withdrawal from my physical affection became more and more apparent. Often when I tried to kiss him, he would turn his face and put his hands up as if defending himself. Finally, I requested a better explanation, whereby Patrick related that when I kissed him, he felt holes were being drilled into his cheeks. How's that for romance?

Physical touch can also be a positive experience. For Patrick, skin-to-skin stimulation can be used as a therapy for relieving stress. A light scratch or a deep muscle massage has a calming effect. To help Patrick relax I sometimes scratch his scalp, arms or back, thereby achieving a healthy physical and emotional response. If he is extremely tense, I use deep muscle therapy, which calms him down considerably. As he becomes calm, his tone of voice changes and his body relaxes. Using touch in a way that Patrick responds to positively has brought closeness in our relationship we both have desired, although at times, thought impossible.

Socializing is a point of genuine frustration for the Asperger person. This area has brought much tension and turmoil into our home, pitting us against each other. Having always been involved in people work, social activities were a "necessary evil" for Patrick. We always assumed we would attend this function or that. When the day arrived, however, Patrick came up with reasons as to why he should not go or how he did not feel up to it. Of course, Jared and I would be encouraged to go, but not having Patrick with us took all the fun out of it. I did not understand the over-stimulation factor, caused by too much time with people, so I created more stress by emotionally pressuring him to go.

Over-stimulation from being around people makes Patrick irritable and an unpleasant person to be around. However, now we have taken action to change this negative drain on our relationship. Together we plan our time in such a way that allows for a balance of social interaction and down time. This allows us both to have our individual needs met. As a couple, we decide which activities we can realistically be involved in, depending on how many demands already are on our time. We try to have realistic expectations. This means that sometimes I go alone, or we all go to an activity, but do not stay long. Patrick and I give ourselves the freedom to cancel out of activities at the last minute, without feeling guilty.

Patrick and I have realized the importance of planning our days to ensure Patrick has enough down time necessary to engage in the people time. Sometimes this means only making a quick presence at functions. Some time ago we attended a wedding, dressing to the hilt and timing our arrival to avoid all the small talk. We stayed long enough to be seen by the parents of the bride talking to a few people to make our presence known. We missed eating the awesome food catered in, but we *did* go together. Other times I have had to make concessions allowing for Patrick to attend functions I want him to go to. Recently, the two of us went to a basketball game. What made it possible for Patrick to go was that he could wear the clothes he had on. He also brought items to work on, giving him an excuse to avoid the social interaction, at the same time allowing him to feel productive. I avoided introducing him to people so he was able to be alone, yet I still enjoyed his company.

Even with the best planning, however, sometimes our plans have to be cancelled. As a couple we have learned to cancel something out of our schedule or pay the price for over-stimulation. We try to avoid Patrick reaching the point of over-stimulation, but sometimes this is unavoidable. When we reach this level, a decision must be made as to what is important for both of us to attend, what I must attend by myself, and what we can cancel altogether. Understanding the amount of stress caused by a lack of balance between people time and down time, together with joint decision-making, takes away the soil for discontentment and allows for richness in our marriage.

Another adjustment made is my acceptance of the role of "social director." I can accept or reject an invitation for our family, depending on whether or not Patrick is ready for people. If this is a necessary social function, I play the part of an extrovert, covering for Patrick's need to withdraw socially. Before attending functions, I check on the food to be served ahead of time. As well, I teach Patrick what to wear for each occasion.

Our family was recently invited to be part of a dinner club in which my social director status came into play. I first gathered as much information as possible by casually asking many questions. This information provided Patrick with a visual of what to expect. We discussed whether or not we could afford the people time, and what would be needed to make our involvement a success. This included such decisions as: not committing to other social activities for an allotted timeframe, having the dinners on a weekend when he would be more relaxed, and trying not to disrupt his schedule. Since Patrick was fairly comfortable with the people involved, that was not a stress to deal with. The time of the dinners and the food being served were the uncontrollable factors. I requested an early dinnertime, and gave the other couples a few days Patrick and I would be available. When the time came for the women to discuss the menu, I was able to make sure Patrick could eat what was planned. With careful planning and consideration, the dinner club was a success.

Clothing can be another battlefield in an Asperger marriage. My dream is that one of these days there will be an Asperger line of clothing. The texture will be soft on the inside, not scratchy at all. These clothes will be extremely comfortable, not necessarily enhancing the person's figure. They will be uniform in nature, plain in color, so as to match everything. The Asperger line will have one pair of pants for dress and another for work. The shirts will all be similar in style. This unique line of clothing would never change or be "upgraded" for marketing purposes. The same stores will always carry this clothing in the same place, and they would never be out of stock. Sound dull? Actually to the wife of an Asperger man, this sounds like the perfect solution!

The topic of clothing used to invoke many unpleasant discussions. Initially, I modernized Patrick's closet with pants and shirts that enhanced his looks. I tried to "make" Patrick wear a variety of clothes he was quite unhappy with. I bought lots of colors and styles of pants and shirts. But though they were indeed his size, when he tried them on, he found them too big, too small, too short, the wrong color or just plain uncomfortable! When Patrick liked something I picked out for him, I would get excited. So to please me, he would wear it every day, until I wished I had never bought the thing!

Patrick really does not care if his clothes don't match. He does not care about colors or styles. In fact, I don't think he even notices, unless the particular item appears "wrong" (like our son's pants dragging on the ground or women wearing men's clothing). What is important is that his clothes are clean, comfortable, and free of holes. If his clothes are not like that, he cannot wear them.

Another stressful issue dealing with clothing is Patrick's inability to change his attire after he has first dressed. Patrick believes that people should put clothes on first thing in the morning, and then change into their bedclothes at night. That's it! There are no variations of this schedule. The trouble comes along when the situation merits different clothing. On a recent weekend Patrick had dressed to work around the house, but shortly thereafter our family was invited to a Super Bowl party. Knowing that it was a good opportunity to spend time with our friends, we went. However, Patrick went "as is," keeping his work clothes on. Fortunately, our friends accepted us for who we were and overlooked the clothes he wore! Other times we have not been so blessed.

Upon our arrival to northern Colorado, Patrick and I attended a social event in our community. All of Patrick's pants were unwearable due to paint, grease, etc. and we had not yet made it to the store to purchase more. (Shopping for clothes is another story!) So there I was all decked out in my dress clothes, while Patrick wore his "spoiled" pants and a nice sweater to meet our new neighbors! I had determined not to be embarrassed. Later, however, my feelings were hurt when a woman commented to me, "I saw you and then I saw him and wondered, 'What could you possibly be doing with that man?'"

A solution for having Patrick fit into the norm a little better is to have a uniform that is agreed upon. His is adaptable to be used for dress, work, or play. Shirts and sweaters, but not pants, are used to make the necessary transitions for various activities. Another remedy is for my dress to be similar to Patrick's, so as not to make his appearance stand out.

Routines or sameness is of extreme importance in the Asperger world. Schedules are the norm and are to be kept and not broken or changed at almost any cost. This structure provides the Asperger person with the ability to function in a world full of "variables."

Preparation for change helps keep the stress level down when situations do have to change. Communicating a possible change in our normal routines is valued. Some areas I bring to Patrick's attention are those such as menu or time changes for dinner and possible upsets in the weekend plans. In December, our son had been asked to be an usher at a wedding. Because the groom was an important figure in our teenage son's life, this was a necessary function to attend. I talked with Patrick ahead of time bringing to his attention the change in his normal schedule. This communication beforehand did not take the stress of the change away, but it did allow for Patrick to be able to make the change. My willingness to help Patrick in this area of his life shows him that I care, thereby deepening our relationship.

Since our days are scheduled, drop in visits can be tough. Although we like to visit with our friends, it is much easier on Patrick if social activities are planned in advance. One day some of our out-of-town friends paid us an unexpected visit. Patrick's world was thrown into a jumble. He had had the whole day planned out, but now it was in disarray. When these situations arise, I jump in as the extrovert I am not, to "cover" for Patrick's unsocial behavior, allowing him to try to regain his structure.

Patrick and I have found some essential keys of communication to help provide marital harmony. These require that I stay on track in story telling and use words as they are defined. Because of my sanguine temperament type, I find this form of communication especially difficult to use. As I get excited, I spew out words, which are extremely confusing to Patrick and only cause to frustrate him. He wants to understand what I have to say, but all he hears is gibberish. Because I love him, I have learned to slow down and think through what I am saying before I let the words flow. I have to think about how my words are coming across to Patrick if I want him to share in my excitement.

One essential key of communication is using words as they are defined. From time to time we have some discussion on what I mean by the words I use. For example, Patrick has asked me what it means for me to *love* him. He wants to love me back as I love him. He must know if we are using the same words in the same way. Because Patrick has a need to trust and believe me, he must understand what I mean by the words I use.

For unstressed communication, I need to stay on track when relaying an event that has happened. This means I must get to the bottom line first, then refrain from using "he said" and "she said" phrases. Using individual names is crucial. If there is more than one of the same first names, I use last names as well. Often I will use something about the person's looks or interests so Patrick can visualize that person. I must also tell the story in the order of events, not jumping to the end or leaving essential parts of the story out. In this way, I stay on track allowing Patrick to understand my communication.

Having time alone is a necessity. If Patrick does not get the time alone he needs, his frustration level slowly builds, without the pressure being relieved. The end result can be damaging to a relationship. The way Patrick fulfills this need is to lie still and alone on the bed, in his favorite chair or on the floor with a pillow with silence and darkness. When he does get time without people, radios or dogs, Patrick becomes peaceful and his head clears.

Early on in our marriage, Patrick always came up with a reason to pull away, be still and quiet, with a T-shirt over his head. He was just resting, thinking or having allergy problems, etc. He knew he needed that time. And I knew if he did not get that time, there would be problems! So, when he had his time alone, he was a nicer guy for it. These days, we try to schedule in that time alone. If Patrick can get the time alone he needs before it becomes an issue, I can still get the interaction I need with him. It works well this way.

For trust to develop there must be total, brutal honesty in a relationship. Without trust, there cannot be a relationship. Patrick would rather have truth even if he does not like what he hears. Eventually, he would find out the truth and the trust would be broken. In our relationship, I need to be completely honest about what I want or need. For example, I need to let Patrick know how often I need hugs or when I need them. I need to tell him how much time I need with him. He is so good about giving me what I want when he knows what I want. But when he doesn't know, he is extremely frustrated because he wants to make me happy.

Our marriage has richness not realized in many relationships. This richness has been developed as Patrick and I have learned how to be successful in the areas of intimacy, socialization, clothing, routines, communication, time alone and trust. Since Asperger Syndrome causes simple events to be quite stressful for Patrick, putting extra effort into these areas has been the cause for the richness we now enjoy.

Patrick's view…

Touch is very powerful. To me, it is either a great experience or an unpleasant one. At times, it feels like being shoved, or poked. There is really no middle ground, at least not much of one. Estelle and I have taught each other how each of us view touch and what it does to us in different situations. I plan to touch Estelle according to how she likes it, not on what I want. I realize she likes a lot of it. I make an effort to touch her non-sexually throughout the day, often. If I make this heartfelt routine a reality, it helps her know I love her. It also prepares her for more passionate touch! Estelle and I hug in the morning and kiss in the afternoon, before and after work. In the evening we often sit in my big chair together; I touch her hand, leg, etc., for a length of time. Brevity does not count when it comes to touching.

Social life can be fun. However, most of the time it is stressful. People do not allow for others to be themselves. One must dress appropriately, have the proper etiquette, clothing, etc... I do not enjoy this game. Often I go only because Estelle wants to. I see it as an act of loyalty and love to her. We prepare for it as Estelle explained.

Clothes are wonderful. Why do "humanoids" get so hung up on matching or styles? Frankly, it seems fake to me. People present themselves the way others want them to. To an Asperger person, this makes no sense. A person is a person, not what they wear. Clothes are bought, sold, traded, and worn out, but soul and character are not. Estelle and I use a "uniform" as she describes it, for her sake. She deserves not to be embarrassed by me. I agree to wear certain clothes for her. My only request is that I only have to wear my uniform. I often think that I would like to dress up more for her; it seems impossible. Sometimes I feel trapped inside my own brain.

Sameness, routine, or lack of change is very helpful in my life. I do like variation within the sameness, sometimes. When we eat pizza out, I will have only cheese for a certain time period. Then I will switch to sausage for a while. To me, that is variation, but to Estelle, variation is different types of food, such as pizza, hamburgers or Chinese food. Food courts at malls are a good place to go when eating out since everyone gets a choice. I'll stick with my routine...

Communication is critical for any relationship. My relationships must have honesty, correct words, and be free from antagonism. Honesty is self-explanatory. "Little white lies" are not acceptable since I will not know what to believe or not believe from someone. Words must always be completely and totally honest. I cannot be close to someone that lies to me; there is no foundation for the relationship. Correct words are words used as defined, or used by the general population. I give the people in meaningful relationships to me more attention and intensity when they talk. Because of that, I pay more attention to detail. If the conversation is frustrating, I would rather not talk. One cannot avoid talking and still keep a relationship.

I do need regular time alone, which is preferred once a day. Absolute darkness and silence is best although sometimes I listen to Morse code to mellow me out. The dits and dahs are like music, beautiful music. This time alone is planned, so as not to interfere with what is important to my family. Usually this is very preventative in nature. If I have sufficient time alone, then I can be nicer to those around me. If not, then my frustration comes out in ways that hurt others.

Talking often and honestly about frustrating areas in our marriage, before getting too frustrated is important. Understanding how each of us views intimacy, socialization, clothing, routines, communication, time alone and trust gives us satisfaction in our relationship. This, in turn, has grown our marriage to be healthy and strong.

4

The Basics of Living
with an Asperger Dad

There are many ways of dealing with a dad that has
Asperger Syndrome (AS). I am going to share some of
them with you from my personal experiences. These
experiences have all been acquired through various years
of living and working with an Asperger parent, my dad.

Feeling

I remember vividly about six years ago I was trying to strip
the plastic casing off some electrical wire so that I could
put an extra light bulb in my room. I had just sharpened
my Swiss army knife to a razor sharp edge. I was using it to
shave off the casing when I slipped and cut my finger
down to the bone. Of course blood was spurting
everywhere and my friend who was there at the time kind
of got sick and panicked at the same time. I got my mom
and got the blood stopped and it fixed up, etc. When my
dad came home from work I told him in detail what had
happened and I had him look at it. During the whole time
he showed no emotion of any kind. He glanced at it and

said something like, "Well, that sounds like it hurt. I hope it feels better," and started eating his supper. I felt really disrespected and hurt and I thought that he should at least feel badly about it. I went away feeling like my dad didn't care at all about me and that I was unimportant.

For some reason the people affected by Asperger Syndrome do not seem to feel as badly or empathize like so called "normal" people. They will look at a situation when somebody gets hurt, see what needs to be done, and do it unemotionally without realizing that the person hurt feels like they don't care. Because they exhibit no emotion during the whole process, the person does not see the actual caring part, instead all he sees is that "I hurt myself and he doesn't even look like he could care less!" Take it from Dad's point of view. He came home from work tired and just wanting to rest. When I showed him my finger he made a huge effort to make sure it was taken care of. He listened to me go on and on, telling him how terrible it was and how much it hurt. He made a show of looking at it and examining it to make me feel better. He even came up with a few suggestions on how to make it heal faster. To him, he did everything in his power to make sure he did his fatherly duty and beyond. He could not understand how I felt unimportant when I came back later and asked him why he didn't care!

One way I have found that helps to deal with this issue is communication. In my opinion, communication is the key for the vast majority of the differences between Asperger people and so-called "normal" people. Simply coming right out and saying calmly and politely what you are thinking and feeling can be a great relief of tension, and reduce the buildup of anger. Of course you have to realize that that is just the way Asperger people are. They can only change so much and it will not be overnight.

Punctuality

Punctuality is a characteristic exhibited in people not affected by the syndrome, but never as extreme as in people that have the syndrome. For example, one day a while ago, I had to go to a guitar lesson after school. I took my guitar and my bicycle and rode out to my teacher's house because it is too far to walk to without taking too long and being late. I got to her house and had my lesson, paid my teacher and walked out the door over to my bicycle. As I put my guitar on top of my bike (it is a small BMX that I still use because it handles nicely), I realized my back tire was flat. I was done with my lesson and I had no more deadlines that night so I decided to walk my bike home. I figured that maybe I would be about half an hour late for supper. I knew that my parents would understand because I couldn't do anything about my tire until I got home. I walked home. It took me about forty-five minutes because I had to go really slow, so that my guitar would not get bumped and get out of tune and so on and so forth. I arrived at my house about thirty minutes late for supper. Right as I pulled my bicycle into the gate and started to unlock the door, my dad and mom pulled up on their motorcycle. I figured that they had gone to the grocery store or something. But as I looked at their faces, I knew that something was wrong. My dad was especially worked up. He tried to be very calm about it, but I could tell that he was furious. He asked me where I had been and what I was doing worrying my mother and him like that. I told him that I had gotten a flat tire and that I came home as fast as possible, but that it took me a long time because I had to deal with both the bicycle and the guitar at the same time. He announced that I was grounded until further notice and that maybe we could talk about it tomorrow morning when he had calmed down. Me, knowing that the best thing was to keep my mouth shut until he had calmed down said, "OK." I put my stuff away and then hung out in my room for the rest of the night, except for when he called me out to question me about what had happened.

Now, not knowing the circumstances about why I was late, many people would say, "Well yeah, I might have been mad too," but now that I have explained them, I hope to illustrate my point. I will compare what happened there with what has happened with my friends' parents when they have done the same exact thing or even worse. My friends' parents have simply said, "Oh OK, I was getting ready to call your friends to see if you had stayed at one of their houses. I'm glad that you are OK. Don't scare your old dad so much!" Whereas, my Dad went looking for me and grounded me for the night.

One thing that I would suggest is that you tell your parent that you might be late even though you are 100 percent sure that you will be home on time. The other thing is that you make all possible effort to be about five minutes early all the time for all occasions, no matter how unimportant, so as to relieve their stress and not get yourself in trouble. It is not like they are holding a double standard. They hold themselves to the same strict punctuality that they hold all their close family members to. They do this because they see you as a part of themselves, and therefore you must obey the same rules as they do. This can have its good sides and it can have its bad sides, but I will get into that more in detail later.

Free days equals work days

One thing about Asperger Syndrome is the need to finish anything and everything that was started. Another thing is the fact that free time or unstructured time, for them, means stress filled time because they don't know what will happen. That is a very hard thing for them. A good example of this is our family workdays. We usually have one free day as a family per week. This day is Saturday because Sunday we all go to church. Saturday time is planned a week in advance. The rough draft of what we will do is already figured out and ready to execute when the day comes around. On the Saturday morning, we get up very early and plan who will do what for the rest of the day. Then we all go do it and meet up sometime later when everybody has finished their assigned task.

Another interesting thing is that they always plan way more than is humanly possible to accomplish. Even if something happens to get in the way of that, they continue even to the point of insanity. For example, last month during Christmas vacation we had about two cords of wood to cut for the day until we were done with our workday. (For those of you who are not familiar with wood terms, a cord is about eight feet long, two feet wide and four feet tall, cut and stacked.) I had just had my wisdom teeth removed the week before. I had a sinus infection from that that I was taking my second set of antibiotics for, as well as the Motrin for the pain and swelling in my mouth. My dad also was sick with some sort of chest infection. My mom had something also, although I don't remember what it was. None of us really should have been working, but my Dad had planned this ahead of time and he was going to get it done. We had borrowed a chain saw from my dad's work and we were using it to cut the logs. The logs were too big for the puny chain saw. We were going to get the wood done so we used it anyway. About two hours through, we had about half of our work done but the logs that were left were the biggest ones. Our chainsaw got very dull and the engine started acting up. We figured that the engine problem might be gas, so we gave it some more gasoline and chain oil. We proceeded to cut the logs but the chainsaw only worked about quarter speed. On top of that, the chain was about as dull as a butter knife. It took us at least fifteen minutes to make one cut out of about two on a log. We really should have quit when the motor messed up, but it was necessary that we finish what we had started. It must have taken us at least another four hours to finish cutting everything. It was like cutting a steak with a butter knife that was just ground, blade first into some pavement.

There is no way to really avoid this. You can only learn to deal with this and understand it so that you will not be so frustrated when something like this happens. You have to realize that they are not doing this to frustrate anybody or to be a jerk, but only that they absolutely have to finish the job, regardless of what happens unless they die or something like that happens. This can be a good thing too, though, because they are very orderly and they also get a lot more accomplished than "ordinary" people do. Our house is much cleaner and is in much better repair than a lot of other people's houses that I have seen because of this quality exhibited in my dad. We get a lot more done in our house in one day than many people get done in a month.

Need to help

Something that ties into this is the Asperger person's need to help people; this is nice if you want to be helped with everything imaginable, but the way in which this help presents itself sometimes can be maddening. The thing that you must realize is that when an Asperger person helps you with something, he will not stop helping you until the job is completely done. This means that even if you want to quit doing something, they will not let you. Also the way that they help you sometimes is in the very strict routines and guidelines of the Asperger mind. The key here is just to tell them if you want them to quit helping you.

Wording

Another interesting thing about Asperger Syndrome is wording and pronunciation. Everything has to be said exactly right. Everybody has to "mean what they say, and say what they mean." A good example was just about half an hour ago when I was on the phone with my dad talking about this chapter. I was telling him that I was going to write about seven pages today. (He knows I am typing it up on my computer, so I automatically assumed that he knew that that was what I was talking about.) He said, "Jared, that's not nearly enough to be a chapter." I said, "Dad, I am talking about seven typed pages, not about actual book pages. It should be at least fourteen, if not twenty book pages." My dad said, "Oh, that's great. I thought you meant book pages." So you see that you have to say exactly what you mean. They take everything literally. I have told my dad things before like, "I am going over to Fred's house, with Fred and Johnny here." He says, "OK, see you in a couple of hours." I leave to go to Fred's house, stop at Johnny's for about ten minutes, and then go to Fred's house and play video games for the afternoon. When I get home Dad gives me this funny look and I realize that I am in trouble, but I don't know why. I have this strange feeling that it has something to do with the fact that I went to Fred's house, but I can't really pin it down completely. He says, "Sit down, Jared; we need to talk." I sit down and he asks me, "What were you doing this afternoon?" I say, "Well, I went over to Fred's house like I told you and we played video games for a while. I really like his James Bond game for his '64. It's really cool." He asks, "What else did you do, Jared?" I say, "I stopped over at Johnny's for about five minutes so that he could tell his mom where he was going and get his

Rainbow Six game so that we could play it at Fred's." "I thought you told me that you were going to Fred's," he says. "Well yeah, that's where I went." "No, you went to Johnny's and then to Fred's," he says.

To me, I was doing what I said because I really did go to Fred's house and that is where I spent the majority of time. So I didn't think that I was doing anything wrong. To my dad, I said that I was going to Fred's house and instead I went to Johnny and Fred's houses. When he tried to call me and I wasn't at Fred's house then that meant that I had lied to him.

The way to avoid this is to always tell your parent to the best extent of your knowledge where you are going. That way even if your friends' parents don't really care, you are still going to be able to go to their house again. I have found that some parents are more strict than others, as far as that's concerned, but usually none of them will be as strict as a parent with Asperger Syndrome.

Another way to avoid miscommunication is to assume nothing. Say everything very literally and make sure that they know what you are talking about. It is not that they are stupid at all. It is rather that you could have an entire conversation with them, then you discover that you were talking about two totally different things completely. Sometimes you may have to ask for their attention to ask them a question. In this case say, "Hey Dad," and wait 'til they answer you. If you don't, you could have to say everything all over again because it may have looked like they were listening, but in reality, they didn't hear a word that you said.

Another interesting thing is that things have to be said the way they remember it. If they remember the hamburger joint in town as Mike's Greasy Burgers and, in reality, the name is Mike's Hamburgers and Fries, then if you don't call it Mike's Greasy Burgers and instead you say, "Let's go to Mike's Hamburger and Fries," he or she will be like, "Where? What are you talking about?" For example, we used to live in an apartment complex a while back called Lunnonhaus. For some reason my dad would always call it Hagendaas. He would always talk about it as Hagendaas, even in front of other tenants and workers at Lunnonhaus. They would always give him the funniest looks like, "Hagendaas, what are you talking about?" It was then that he would realize that he had said something wrong. Again, it is not at all that they are stupid. It is just the way that they think and remember things.

Commitment/loyalty

One of the best things about people with Asperger Syndrome is the fact that they are loyal and committed. They have a much better sense of commitment and they are also much better lifelong friends than other people. A good example of this is when I got in a fistfight at a church when I was about six years old. It was at AWANA's (a Bible club for kids) and there was this kid there who wouldn't leave me alone. I told him on numerous occasions to leave me alone and that I would punch him if he didn't. He did not listen to me and so I punched him right there in front of God and everybody. His nose started bleeding and so on and so forth. The AWANA leaders gave me a real hard time and lectured me on the verse about turning the other cheek, and how what I had done was so terrible, and how I needed to ask forgiveness from the kid and from God also. I was scared because I was afraid that what they were saying was true, and how terrible it was to get kicked out of church. They called my parents and then they came and they talked to the head AWANA dude. My dad had told me earlier that if the kid kept bothering me, that I was to give him good warning and then pop him in the nose. My dad told this dude that, and he told him that I was right for doing that and also that it was not my fault that I was just obeying my parents and that if he had a problem with it that he would have to talk to my dad about it and leave me alone. I don't remember the exact details, but the dude backed down and left me alone and he did not end up kicking me out like he was going to do. That is a good example of Asperger loyalty. My dad was willing to stand up to this guy. He knew that what I did was right, even though he knew that it might make him look bad and that some of his adult Christian friends would think that he was a moron. He was willing to take the rap so that I wouldn't have to, and he did not back down.

You don't really want to prevent this commitment and loyalty, so my advice would be to enjoy it. The only time that it is a bad thing is when they have decided to help you with something that you do not want help with. This can sometimes be annoying, but it also shows you that they love you. A way to deal with this is to tell them straight up, "Hey dad, I appreciate you wanting to help me build my model airplane, but to tell you the truth I really want to do it myself. If I need help, is it okay if I call you and ask you to give me some advice?" That is much better than just ignoring their efforts at helping you and just hoping that they go away, because they won't. They will just get more and more frustrated, and that will make them want to help you even more.

Routines

One interesting thing about people with Asperger Syndrome is that everything has to be in the right place and stay there unless they are notified that it was moved. There must be a good reason for it to be moved. The only exception to this rule is if they move it. This only applies to their personal stuff. As far as the rest of the world, it must be neat and orderly, but it does not have to be immaculate and under keen surveillance. For example, our house has to be swept and mopped on a weekly basis. The trash and the vacuuming have to be done daily. My room is kind of considered a "no-zone" where he psychs himself up before he comes in. And his side of their bedroom is all nice and picked up, and my mom's is normal.

He also has his routines that he started, God knows how long ago, that he still follows. He gets up at four in the morning, plans the day, does his quiet time, takes his shower and then gets to work at about six fifteen to six thirty, when he has to be there at seven o'clock. To "normal" people this may seem crazy, but it keeps him sane. If he does not have these routines, or if one of them gets messed up, it stresses him out beyond belief. If this happens, then he has to fix it, or the rest of his day is ruined.

For example, let's say that it is a family workday and he has decided that every picture in the house has to be hung. About halfway through he runs out of nails, screws, whatever. He has to get the pictures hung, so he has to get more nails. He goes to the store to get the nails. They are out. He goes to another store. They don't carry that type. He goes to the last store, and it is closed. He has to have those pictures hung somehow by the end of the day, so he decides to use four inch long roofing nails, because that is the only thing that he can find. They really are not noticeable from the front or the sides if they are pounded in well enough. So, the job is not done, but enough work has been done as to make it okay to fix it tomorrow when better nails can be purchased. Another example is if he forgot to set his alarm and he woke up an hour late. To us, that would be no big deal. We would still have plenty of time to get to work and we would do our quiet time later when we got home. But for him, it ruins his whole day because his routine has been broken. He is angry with himself for forgetting to set the alarm and also angry that he will have to disrupt even yet another routine so that he can fix the one that he has broken.

My advice would be to make sure you never have any part in breaking any of their routines in the slightest. Even if it seems like a five-minute disruption would not matter, it does. Avoid bothering them while they are in the middle of their routines.

Well, I have shared some of the most important things that I have learned from living with my Asperger dad for seventeen years. I hope that after reading this chapter, you will have gained some insights and some valuable coping skills for living with a parent that has Asperger Syndrome. In the next chapter, I am going to discuss some of the issues that may arise as you grow through different stages in your life. Don't let these potholes become a roadblock in your relationship with your parent. Instead, use them as stepping-stones towards a stronger relationship and better communication.

5

The Three Stages of Growth with an Asperger Parent

When I was growing up, my dad having Asperger Syndrome (AS) affected me. I went through three specific time periods in which I learned to deal with him differently. The first of these was junior high. (Before that, I didn't realize my dad's differences were as dramatic as they really are, so my comments would be totally useless.) Anyway, until eighth grade I had no idea that my dad had AS, so it was rather frustrating because I had nothing to assign his abnormalities and extreme need for structure to. I first started noticing this need for structure when I was in the 6th grade. I noticed that when he came home, not only was he tired physically, he was also "peopled out." I also noticed that he needed everything to be in order so that he could relax and accomplish things. I was the complete opposite way. I did not want things in my room in order and I often got bored because of the lack of people around to get sick of.

His need for structure was very difficult and puzzling for me as a kid, because I did not understand why everything had to be so rigid and structured. I also had trouble understanding why he was so sick of people. On the weekends, all he would want to do was stay home and relax, while working with only our family. In a way it helped me to become more social and a whole lot more disorganized.

I saw routines and structure in my dad and I decided that I would not impose strict rules like that on myself. I really did not have to deal with these routines and patterns of organization myself; I just observed them. This was nice because I could just sit back and observe them at a distance. My response to this was to become less and less organized, and I began to follow less and less routines. You may well have experienced this yourself in response to your AS parent. I do not think that this is the best solution, because obviously you need to have some organization and routines in your life. However, it is nice to be able to relax and enjoy life, and not be caught up in excessive routines. You just have to learn what you can from your AS parent, and decide for yourself.

When I began high school, I really started to be affected by my dad's differences. The thing that I was first affected by was his need for punctuality. I would be hanging out with my friends and I would come home five minutes late. I did not think that it was a big deal, and my friends and their parents did not think so either, but to my dad it was an enormously big deal. I would end up getting grounded for a couple of days just because of this.

A lot of the reason that it bothered my dad so much was that it broke a routine when I would come home late. As I have mentioned in the previous chapter, breaking a routine for an Asperger person causes serious frustration for them. This is very hard for the kid because he has to be home exactly on time, so when his friend says, "Hey, I gotta run by the store real fast and buy some Pepsi, iz that kool?" Then you say, "I gotta be home at five which gives us ten minutes. If we go, I will be late." And then your friend says, "You will only be like two minutes late, tops. What's the big deal, are you going to turn into a pumpkin or something?"

At this point you have three choices (really two, but let me explain). You can say, "Alright, dood. That's kool. I am sure that my dad/mom will not mind" (a complete lie), and go home making sure that your neck muscles are nice and loose so that when the blade separates your body from your head, you will die painlessly. Or you could answer, "Well you see, my mom/dad has something called Asperger Syndrome. It is a Pervasive Developmental Disorder, which is characterized mostly by an extreme need for structure. This includes a very real need to keep routines. To deviate from one of these routines is very frustrating for them. If I were to come home late, I would be causing the aberration of one of these routines, thus causing extreme frustration aimed at me. So, if you do not want to see my head stuck to the top of the telephone pole in front of my house tomorrow morning, then I suggest that we just skip the trip to the store." This answer would work, but among other things, by the time you got done explaining this to your friend, you would already be late. The best answer is answer is: "Well, my mom/dad is really obsessed with time, and if I don't get home exactly on time I will get in big trouble. So, if you want to go to the store that is fine, but I have to go home now." This third solution is much better than the first two, but your friend will probably still not be that happy about it. If you hang out with them a lot, then they will get to know you and they will understand what is going on and they will plan for you to leave earlier than them, thus easing frustration.

Another thing that was also different from my friends and their households was how we celebrated holidays. For most people a holiday means a day to relax and just kind of do fun stuff and sit around. It means just doing whatever you feel like at the moment, just kind of playing things by ear. It is a time to get away from the normal, hectic schedules and having to run here and there and do this and that. Well for an Asperger person, a lack of structure means disaster and mass confusion as well as frustration. So for them, even a holiday must be structured.

The difference is that the structure may contain times for the family members to do nothing productive. Of course, the Asperger person himself is incapable of doing nothing so he will plan things to do. Aside from that, the holiday is very strictly scheduled. Usually it will be explained to you a couple of days ahead of time so that you will know what to do when the time comes. An example of a Christmas Day schedule might be like this: at 7am we will open presents, at 7.30 we will clean up the wrapping paper, then at 8am we will eat breakfast. After that we will take showers until 9am. At 9am we will go outside and make snowmen until 10am. At 10am, we will come inside and drink hot chocolate until 10.30. From 10.30 until 11am, we will eat candy. At 11am, we will start getting ready to go to the Case's to eat lunch. At 11.30, we will leave for the Case's. At 12pm, we will get there and eat until… Now they may not explain all of this to you in detail, but it is in their head. If you ask them, "Hey, Mom/Dad, is it kool if I go hang out with Joe from 10 to 11am?", then you will find out that they really do have everything planned out.

This scheduling of holidays is something that will stick out to your friends also. They will have a hard time understanding how it is possible to have your holiday planned a week or two in advance. It will also bug them that they will have to ask you far ahead of time in order to hang out with you. The best thing to do when they ask you what your problem is, is to tell them that your parent is very strict as far as stuff like that goes and there is nothing that you can do about it. If you do not give them a good explanation as to what "your problem is," then they will think that you just do not want to be friends with them and they will stop trying to be your friend. In short, holidays can be very fun times and very frustrating ones. The difference between the two is communication and understanding between you and your AS parent.

One thing that also affected me was the way that my dad handled having fun. To him, as with all things, fun must be structured. To me, the definition of something fun is unstructured. If I really want to have fun, I just kind of fly by the seat of my pants and do what I feel like when the time is right. If I structure fun more than just basic plans, it just becomes another task that must be completed, rather than something that I am looking forward to doing. Well, it is just the opposite for my dad. If something is fun, it must be structured or else it is frustrating and confusing.

So, as with many things that you have to adjust to when you have an Asperger parent, you need to find a middle ground, or way to adjust to this. When having fun and doing things as a family, you will just have to accept the fact that they are going to be planned out extensively. Just relax and enjoy it! When you are with your friends you can do it the way you want. You can also talk to your parent and tell them, "I just want you to plan some time where I do not have to accomplish anything at all. I just want to be able to do nothing; to me that is fun. If I try to accomplish things, it takes the fun out of it." Chances are, if you do not tell them this, they are not going to have any idea that when you have fun, you do not try to accomplish anything. You see, for them, accomplishing things is fun. In order to have fun, they must be accomplishing something, no matter how trivial.

Something that ties into this is when you want to spend time with your AS parent. Again, you have to find something that you both like to do. Find something to do where they can accomplish something and you can just sit around and not do anything. This may sound impossible, but believe me, you will find something if you talk to them about it.

Something that also really started to affect me was how my dad fell into play with my friends and my relationships with my friends. Asperger people are very loyal and committed to their family members. Well, part of the way that my dad's commitment to me showed, was in dealing with my friends. He made a rule that he had to meet my friends before I hung out with them a lot. This is just an example of something that your parent could do that might affect your social life with your friends. It was often embarrassing to me to have to say, "Yeah, that's kool, I would like to hang out at your house tomorrow, but first you have to come over and meet my dad cause he always wants to meet my friends." Every parent is different, but it is highly likely that your parent will create a set of rules involving your friends that will likely involve embarrassment for you. The thing is, they might not realize how embarrassing it really is for you because of their lack of sensitivity to what other people think. Because of this, they will most likely create rules that will ratchet your "koolness" down way below the healthy level. Rules like the one my dad had about meeting my friends made things difficult for my friends and me, but sometimes, you just have to roll with it. I eventually started talking to my dad about things like this. We worked on adjusting them, so that it would be easier to hang out with my friends and not look stupid as I did before.

Now that I am in college, things have changed a lot, but my quest for complete freedom has not yet been achieved. I am seventeen, so I am not legally an adult, but all of my friends are at least eighteen so that can be interesting at times. However, dealing with my dad as far as education is concerned has changed a lot. When I was in high school, my dad was always asking me about school. I had to give him report cards when they came out and I got grounded for bad grades. Anyway, now that I am older, education is in my hands and that has been a journey all its own. Now, however, the main issue is staying out late with my friends. My dad's normal routine is to go to bed at eight or nine and for me to get home about eleven from work, and go to bed about then.

When I started asking to go out with my friends until one thirty, you can imagine that I got some raised eyebrows. Not only is it a change in routine, from an "adult's" perspective, that is late for a seventeen-year-old to be out. At first he did not want me to be out past midnight. Then when he realized that I was responsible enough to stay out later, and he got used to the change in routine, he started letting me stay out later. If you are in the same predicament that I was/am in, then my best advice to you is to get your parent used to the change slowly. Change for an AS person takes lots of time and energy. Let them get used to it for a while or you will not get anything that you want.

Overall, living with an AS parent has been a challenge as well as an excellent growing experience. It certainly has its ups as well as its downs. I regret the fact that I had to focus on the negative aspects of this parent–child relationship, but the only things that I could foresee your needing advice on were the things that created problems.

6

An Even Closer Look
at the Asperger Parent

In this chapter, we are going to look even closer at the parent with Asperger Syndrome (AS) than we did in my two earlier chapters. I will discuss some of the same issues that I talked about there, and I am going to bring up some more detailed issues as well.

Structure

An important part of learning how to effectively live and work with an AS person is to understand them as beings that sometimes act like cyborgs. They are human in appearance and principle, but the way that they think is oftentimes like a robot. Everybody has seen those cheesy seventies and eighties TV shows where there is some evil invincible robot that must be destroyed. The hero in the story then devises a plan to make the robot short circuit by feeding it information that it cannot compute. It then slowly dies, chanting the uncomprehendable string of information as it melts into the floor.

This scenario is extreme but in milder terms this sort of thing does happen to people with AS. But instead of melting they may get very frustrated, angry, or, depending on the circumstance, they may suffer silently losing many a night of sleep to the frustrations of not understanding "humanoids" or of having their structure broken. This may sound outrageous at first, but I assure you that as you learn to understand an AS person having routines much like a robot or a computer, it will make your life with your AS parent much easier.

Routine is defined in *The Random House College Dictionary* as: 1) a customary or regular course or procedure; 2) regular or unvarying. A routine is necessary for Asperger people in every aspect of life. In order to brush their teeth they even have to have a certain routine or procedure that they follow. For example, in the morning the AS person gets up at a certain time, and grabs his toothbrush, being sure not to put water on the toothbrush until he has closed the cabinet doors. He then puts paste on the brush and begins to brush his teeth starting at the back lower teeth, then moving to the sides of the back teeth then the inside of the back teeth, then to the middle set of teeth to repeat the whole process all over again until he has finally finished. He might not even realize that a pattern exists here, but nevertheless, it does exist. My point in explaining this is to emphasize the fact that an AS person's life is one big routine broken down into smaller routines.

So you may say, "Great, how is that supposed to help me with my AS parent and my relationship with him?"

The thing that you must realize is that everybody has routines; that is not the important part here. The thing that you must understand is the importance and the need for routines that AS people have. They simply cannot live without structure. What you must learn is to never break any of their routines for almost any reason, unless it is an emergency.

The disruption of a routine for the AS person can cause extreme frustration. To us, if we get our routines broken, we fix them and go on with our day. For them it is a much bigger deal. The disruption of one routine creates a domino effect, disrupting many routines until the AS person can't fix them. In order to fix one routine, s/he must break another one.

For example, if I was an AS person my morning routine would be to wake up at 5am, get out of bed from 5 to 5.10am, eat Frosted Flakes from 5.10 to 5.30am and get dressed and be ready for work from 5.30 to 6am. Then if my alarm went off at 5.10 instead of 5am, I would have to spend ten minutes less eating Frosted Flakes, which means that I would not have enough time to read the paper while eating, and ten minutes less to plan my day out.

This may seem like a very trivial thing to you or me. However to an Asperger person, these changes in events are earth shakers. I do not understand this fully, but even a miniscule change in an AS person's structure will cause them great stress and frustration. The interesting thing about this is that nobody will notice any signs of distress, except for the immediate family of the person. The reason for this is that the AS person sees his family as an extension of himself; therefore everything that is expected by the person himself is expected for the family. The Asperger person has to work very hard to fight this urge off, although s/he fully realizes that the family members are independent and their own persons. This can often cause conflict, because most people do not want to be subjected to the strict expectations that the person with Asperger Syndrome has put on him or herself.

Working with your AS Parent

In an earlier chapter, I talked about working with my AS parent, my dad. I am now going to expand on this concept and cover it a bit more in detail. Working with an Asperger person is just like any other routine, it must not be broken, and it must be completed regardless of the consequences. This means that a certain amount of work must be accomplished in order to complete the routine, regardless of the circumstances.

In some cases the AS person's need for completion will seem extreme or obsessive-compulsive to almost any observer. It will also definitely seem extreme to the non-AS person involved in the work. The Asperger person must also have everything done *exactly right*. To me, for example, "right" would mean that the window I am cleaning must be clear with no spots or smudges on it, (at least none that can be seen with the naked eye). For a person with Asperger Syndrome, it must not have any remote trace of dirt or dust particles that could be viewed with an electron microscope. Believe me, if you think that

I am joking, try it out on your AS parent. Clean something the best you can, then ask him/her to look at it to make sure that it is clean. Then you will see what I am talking about. With just a seemingly cursory glance, all of your mistakes will be revealed. The best thing to do is to make your work experience with your AS parent as pleasurable as possible, because the odds are, you are not going to want to work.

There are some things that you will want to remember about Asperger people, one being that they love to teach. My dad, for example, loves to teach everybody and anybody. I personally think that an excellent profession for an AS person would be teaching of some sort, but that is just my opinion. Anyways, if you ask an AS person about one of his possessions and how it works, plan to be there for at least an hour. Say, for example you ask your dad about his new riding mower and how it works. He will then proceed to launch into a teaching session about each little part and how it works and how exactly you should use it when cutting grass at a certain height at a specific time of day and so on. By the end, you will have received a sales pitch that will rival the riding mower company's top salesman. Now you may be saying, "Well, that's what all guys do." I can tell you for sure that it goes beyond the person's excitement over the purchasing of a new possession. When it happens to you, you will know what I am talking about. Now you may think, "Well that's good, I love to learn."

It is always good to learn new things. However, sometimes you really do not have the time for an hour-long teaching session with your parent. You would much rather be doing something productive with your friends. There are ways to express your need to move on without being rude and disrespectful. The key thing to understand here is that Asperger people might not notice signs that you would like to leave like most people will. They are very good at paying attention to detail, but when they are in the middle of teaching you about something, all of their attention is focused on teaching, not on paying attention to you.

There are some things to remember when trying to get out of these situations. The first one is to not ask *any* questions. To an AS person, asking questions means that you are very much interested and that you would like to know more, prompting them to spew out even more information. A second thing to do is to wait until they stop momentarily and then sum up what they have been saying. For example you could say, "Well that is interesting that you can cut hedges as well as six foot tall grass. I will have to check that out the next time I mow the yard, (pause) but I really have to go now because Fred and Jill are waiting for me to go roller blading. We have to go now if we want to get back by the time it is dark." This shows that you have learned something (by summing up what he told you), thus helping him to feel like he has taught you something and accomplished something and that he was not just wasting his time. It also allows you politely to tell him that you are done and that you need to leave. Saying other things like, "Ok, that's nice. Wow!" and stuff like that will get you nowhere. If he thinks that you are just going to sit around, then forget ever leaving because Asperger people hate it when their kids are just sitting around doing nothing.

With AS people, you have to say exactly what you mean. When you say, "Yes, uh huh" etc., they will think that you want them to go on and keep talking. When dealing with your parent in a situation like this, sometimes it is impossible to get out of the situation, and you will just have to deal with it. Some suggestions would be to mention homework, the need for food or water, or something else that they will understand the importance of. But, remember if they let you go do one of these things, then you had better do it because you can be very sure that they will remember if you try to trick them or say one thing and do another. If you mess up one time, your chances for the next time will diminish greatly.

Something that I have noticed about AS people is their need to always be doing something. It must also always be in order and executed as planned. At the beginning of the day, my dad will always have everything planned out to the smallest detail of all that he is going to accomplish. If he comes upon unexpected free time, he will immediately plan what he can get done during that period. It is impossible for him to not do anything.

Details

AS people can pick out, remember, and fix detailed things (that would be considered difficult for us), with great ease. This can be a very positive side of the syndrome. However, if the person with AS happens to be your parent, then this attention to detail can be a very "unkool" thing, and it can turn into a downside very quickly. An example of the upside of this detail obsession is an old lock that I have. I have an old combination lock that I hadn't used for five years. One day I decided to use it for something, so I pulled it out hoping that the combination would be written on it somewhere because I had long since forgotten it. When I pulled it out, there was no combination on it anywhere, so I decided to ask my dad if he remembered where we put the combination. I told him what was up, and it took him about thirty seconds to remember the combination.

An example of a downside that it might present is, when you do not do something that you are supposed to take care of. For example, if your parent tells you to make sure that you cut the grass, and put the grass clippings in a red bag (after you have carefully combed out all the dirt and debris with a rake), label the bag "grass," and give it to the neighbor, Bob. S/he also tells you to make sure that you give your pet elephant, Fido, some peanuts before you leave. Well, you decide to do all of the above, except you give Fido some cashews that *you* were supposed to eat, instead of the peanuts. You may think that your parent will never notice. But s/he will see that Fido snorts twice as long when he gets home, but when you give him peanuts; he only snorts half as long. You will be sure to hear about it when you get home!

For some reason Asperger people can pick out the smallest details in anything. Their eyes are like binoculars. Everything that they see gets magnified so that they can pick apart even the most complex entity. For them to relax, every detail must be right and in order. To them, relaxation is having everything (down to the exact detail) go as planned in their routines. Details form the base of an Asperger person's life. Without details, there would be nothing to base their numerous routines upon. To the AS person, details keep life manageable as well as understandable. This is why they are so organized, and they have exceptional skills in detail work. When you are working with them, even around the house, you will see that they are seemingly obsessed with making sure that every detail is correct.

What others think

Another interesting thing about people with AS is that they, for the most part, do not care about what other people think about them. For some reason or another, Asperger people figure that as long as they are OK to themselves, then it really doesn't matter what other people think of them. This can lead to many odd situations. For example, recently I learned of my dad's wish for a motorcycle tool kit for his Father's Day present. Now, normally people give you a few ideas of what they want for a present and then let you get whatever you think that they would like most. With my dad this is not so. He wants to know exactly what he is getting so that he can make sure that it has what he needs. He picks it out, and then I buy it for him.

One day, he was looking at this kit in a catalog and it did not say what size Allen Wrenches® or hex keys that it had in it; all it said was "assorted sizes." So after about twenty minutes of talking, with two different people on the phone at the selling company, I finally got him all the information that he wanted (or so I thought). Most people would not call to get every detail about the sizes. They would just ask if the kit had a certain size of this or that and then be done, but with Asperger people the need for detail is absolutely necessary. After I hung up, however, my dad then wanted to know the name brands of the tools. Specifically, he wanted to know if the adjustable wrench was made by Crescent® and if Vise-Grip made the clamp pliers. When I called back to ask these questions, the man I was talking to told me that I was free to ask all the questions I wanted. He said that a customer had just called and asked a bunch of questions and the kit was still spread all over his desk. The funny part about this was that *I* was the previous customer who had just called! The whole point in sharing this story with you is to illustrate the fact that my dad did not care what the people on the other end of the phone thought of us. I, on the other hand, was worried about what they thought of us and I was hoping that they didn't call the cops on us for harassment or something.

This insensitivity to what others think also manifests itself in other ways. For example, when your parent is talking to you in front of your friends, he may say, "Jared that shirt looks like a girl's shirt. Why don't you go and put something else on?" Now, that is a horrible thing to say to someone in front of his or her friends, but your parent might not realize that. They just assume that since it would not matter to them, then it must not bother you and certainly must not affect what your friends think about you. In order to avoid further embarrassment you have to tell them that this bothers you ahead of time, instead of afterwards after the damage has already been done. Tell them to explain stuff like that to you in private when your friends are not around. Tell them that your friends made fun of you for two months after that incident with the shirt. They will not figure this out for themselves; you will have to tell them this.

One thing that ties into this is the fact that our AS parent embarrasses us in front of our friends because of the way that they look, act, and dress. Our friends may think that they are strange or odd. Again, you have to ask your parent to not do certain things in front of your friends. Sometimes they are just going to do it anyways and it may not have anything to do with the fact that they have Asperger Syndrome. They may just be old and not understand the extreme "koolness" that we youngsters possess. ☺

Another way that they might embarrass you is their obsession with details. They may tell you that you really need to fix your pants because they are dragging on the floor; all while your friends are listening. They may also insist that you be home at exactly six o'clock to eat dinner and then you can leave again, only to come back home an hour later to do homework and go to bed.

This might bother you because your friend Bob's dad just says to be home at seven, so that you can eat and do homework afterwards or at the same time, as long as you get it done. You can talk to your parent about this but s/he will most likely not back down, because it is in his/her routine to eat supper at six so therefore you must eat supper at six. Now if you ask him to change his routine so that he knows that every night you will eat supper and do homework at seven, then he might agree to that. Ask him to also tell you stuff like when you have to be home in private, that way it is less embarrassing to you and you do not look like a little kid in front of your friends. If you explain this stuff to him, he will most likely be willing to do this for you, but if you do not do this then s/he will have no idea how quickly it yanks down your "koolness" factor.

Communication

This brings up another interesting point about AS: *communication is very important*. Communication is perhaps the most vital part of living with an Asperger person in harmony. You see, a lot of times people with AS do not pick up on things that the rest of us would think are obvious. For instance, I might think that my dad knows that I am hungry because I have worked six hours with no food. But unless I tell him that I am going to fall down and die unless I eat within the next thirty seconds, the thought that I am hungry will not even cross his mind. People with AS do not feel things like we do. For this reason, it is absolutely essential to communicate with your Asperger parent and tell him things like this. A good thing that I have learned is to ask him what the best way to talk to him is. If you want something from your parent, like most if not all of us do, then there are several steps to follow to help ensure your success:

- Make sure everything is in order. This means that you need to have all of your chores done, homework finished and all other assigned jobs done. This is the most important one. If things are out of order for an AS person, then they must be put in order at all costs, meaning that you will have to finish those things immediately.

- Say exactly what you mean. This means that if you want to go chill with your friends at the movie theatre at 5pm Eastern Standard Time, then you had better say exactly that when asking for permission to go. If you hint at what you would like to do or give unspecified times, your request will be turned down.

- Make your point quickly. Asperger people hate it when you talk a lot, exaggerate, or in any way take too long to tell them what you need. If you tell them that you just want to talk to them about nothing in particular then they will be fine. But if you don't, they will get frustrated waiting for you to make your point.

One thing that I have learned to do is to provide my dad with the four Ws: who, what, where, and when. I tell him this right off the bat before I add anything else:

- Who I am going to be with. This means people that my dad already knows and has met.

- What I am going to be doing. This includes a mini-itinerary of exactly what I am going to be doing at specific times.

- Where I am going to be. This is so that if he needs to get a hold of me, then he will have no problem doing so.

- When I am going. This also includes when I am going to get back from what I am doing.

If you tell them all these things *before* you meet up with your friends, then you will save yourself the embarrassment of being asked this stuff in front of them.

Something that will also be helpful to you is to understand that AS people need to have check in times with their kids. These are a way to keep everything in order for the Asperger person. They need to have times to just sit down and have you tell them how everything is going and what you have accomplished like you were supposed to, as well as what you did not get done and why and how you are going to get it done. They will also probably ask you how things are going in your life and stuff like that. The trick is to get these out of the way at your convenience, instead of theirs. If you wait for them to ask you to check in, it will most likely be at a very inopportune time for you. I had one at 5.30am the other day because I did not volunteer myself for one earlier. If you like getting up at five in the morning then that is great, but I like to sleep.

These are the most basic skills that you will need in order to effectively ask what you want from your AS parent. Remember, always wait a day or two to ask for something, right after you have gotten yourself into trouble.

Frustration

One of the most important and difficult subjects to cover is how to deal with your parent when s/he is angry with you. Inevitably, even if you are the best kid in the world, you will get into conflict with them sometime, so I am going to give you some guidelines to follow in conflict.

One important thing to remember is that when an Asperger person gets angry, it can go from being very small (frustration) to being very big (anger) in a short amount of time. You often have very little warning, and it can be very surprising or bewildering to the unsuspecting person. The key to calming the situation down is to remain calm yourself. If you get upset, it will only get worse and your parent's frustration will rise, causing the situation to escalate.

A critical skill to learn is to teach yourself to recognize the telltale signs that indicate that that you are putting wood on the fire. I have become angry with my dad because all of a sudden he would freak out and become all upset over the littlest thing imaginable. I eventually explained this to him and he said, "Well, it is an accumulation of things and that one little thing is the straw that breaks the camel's back. If you look carefully you will notice that there are signs that an explosion is coming." For example, on Sunday I could not take out the trash, on Tuesday I could not brush the dog, and on

Wednesday I could not close the shed doors all the way. By the time Friday rolls around and I forgot to check the mail, my dad will be very frustrated with me and almost any little thing I do wrong will set him off.

Now this may not be obvious because your parent will appear to not be bothered at all and they may not even say anything to you until it all builds up. Then you can be sure that you will hear about it! When you get home from school Friday night you will notice the difference in your parent by the way he talks or doesn't talk to you, and how he is acting towards you. Now when s/he sits you down to talk about your transgressions, be sure to not have an attitude, because s/he will notice that and it will just add more wood to the already sky high fire. The first thing to do if you want to get it over with quickly is to take responsibility for what he is saying that you did and apologize appropriately. If you do not do that, then cancel your plans for the night because he will not let you go until you have logically gone through each step that you took to commit the crime and you have acknowledged your guiltiness. Now the chances are high that you are not going to agree with what your parent is saying, so tell him that, but make sure you explain why and do so respectfully.

Do not make a bunch of excuses because that will make him/her angrier and your sentence harder. Remember that AS people function on logic, and they especially revert to it when they experience an emotional disturbance! So remember to make your defense as logical as possible, and it will go much smoother for you. The clearer that your parent understands what you are trying to get across to them, the better for you it is, because it means that they will be less frustrated.

These are some practical ideas to remember when dealing with an angry AS parent. These guidelines are not a "get out of jail free" card; rather they are a guidebook to follow in order to make your stay easier. The point I am trying to make is, if you are in trouble, you are not going to get out of it, so just remain calm. Your parent will not get more frustrated, thus keeping you from digging yourself a bigger hole than you are already in.

Asperger people's friends

The way that an Asperger person's friends view him/her can be very interesting as well. It usually takes a long time, about a year or so, until a person is accepted into the person's strict circle of friends. An AS person's friends are usually far and few between, but they are true friends. The way that you, the AS person's kid, fall into this is that at times you may need to interpret your parent to their friends. Many times it is likely that your parent's friends will be perplexed by your parent's sometimes strange behavior. For example, there might be a very important social function that your parent might really want to attend. However, your parent might be "peopled out." The definition of "peopled out," according to Jared's "Dictionary of Asperger Terms" is: a condition character-ized by extreme physiological delusions. These delusions appear in the form of visions. The most common of these visions is a view of the patient's skull exploding. This condition also produces extreme fed-up-ness with the species homosapiens. This fed-up-ness is also commonly accompanied by visions of solitary islands or dark caves where the patient may escape discovery by the species homo sapiens. These delusions are brought about by the expenditure of large quantities of time spent in the company of the species homo sapiens.

Because of these symptoms, your parent might be forced to cancel going to this important event. Your place in this might be to explain why this great tragedy has occurred. It might be rather difficult to explain, so if you do not have much time just simply explain that your parent is not feeling well so s/he cannot come, even though they were really looking forward to it. If it is somebody that you know really well and who is competent in the knowledge of the term "peopled out" then you must tell him/her that this is what happened in this case. The reason that you might need to do this is because your parent may not tell them him/herself. Try working with your non-AS parent to explain these things to your parent's friends.

To illustrate my point I will end this chapter with a story from my own experience. One time when we were living in the Dominican Republic, our Dominican friend invited us as a family over to his house for a nice dinner. He was really a friend of my dad's, but he wanted us to come over as a family to eat with his family. We planned this dinner for a couple of weeks in advance, and when the time came to go my dad was all peopled out. So my mom and I went. When we got there he and his wife were all dressed up, and he had made some nice rabbit stew, from some of his rabbits that he had raised himself. He noticed that my dad was not with us and he asked where he was. My mom and I informed him that he would not be able to make it because he was not feeling well. This hurt our friend's feelings greatly, but not as much as it would have if we did not interpret my dad to him. The moral of the story is that whenever possible, you must interpret your parent to his/her friends. That way they can understand that your parent is not being rude, just suffering from unavoidable circumstances.

These are just some of the many things that you will come into contact with when dealing with your Asperger parent. Learning how to communicate with your parent will help you solve almost any problem that will arise. I hope that this advice will come in handy for you when you are dealing with your Asperger parent. Just remember, the key is to *communicate.*

I hope that these three chapters, as well as the entire book, will help you in dealing with your parent that has Asperger Syndrome. The journey to understanding your parent can be difficult at times, but if you wish to have a relationship with your parent, it is a task that must be undertaken.

7

Raising a Child While Enjoying Each Other

Wow! You just got an earful from our son in the last three chapters! It's hard not to notice his candor and flare for words. In this chapter, we're going to talk about how Estelle and I work together in raising this young man. My Asperger Syndrome adds another dimension to what is already seen by some as a daunting task.

It is quite amazing how two people can view the same incident in radically different ways. To keep sanity in our home, Estelle and I have created a few tools, giving us all a good foundation to build on. Now, we will discuss how Estelle and I give Jared a vision for life and show him how to get there. We will explain our process of interpretation of each other to Jared. We will show how we live out well-defined roles as Mom and Dad. The benefit of inter-personal communication will also be considered as it concerns areas of friction and certainly the major issues regarding Jared.

Estelle gives Jared the vision and I show him how to get there. This is accomplished by taking opportunities to exclaim his great potential. His mother tells him to run for president and she specifies his talents and abilities. Estelle gently reminds him to pursue the career he wants, but makes sure he knows how great he is. I, however, go through the mechanics of the 'hows' with him.

It's my job to show Jared how to get to college by sending away for catalogs and visiting the campuses with him. I stand with him while he gets his bank account, driver's license, or faces the principal. I do not do the hard things for him, but I go through the process with him. I frequently give my son the guidance he needs to protect him through the process. If he needs to fail, I allow him to do so, while showing him my support.

When Estelle and I interpret each other to Jared, we are often diffusing anger, frustration, or misunderstanding. As our son is told things he does not like, or one of us notices his frustration, we approach him gently. When Jared has had conflict with one of us, the other will give him time to calm down. Then we will approach him on his turf, in a place comfortable to him. Estelle or I listen to the frustration and other emotions Jared needs to express, but we do not allow him to talk poorly about the other spouse. If he disrespects one of us, we simply remind him that we are there to love and support him, but not to take sides with him. Our purpose is simply to let Jared express his emotions and views and gently try to help him understand the other parent's viewpoint. The intent is simply to interpret each other to Jared, not try to force him to accept what we have to say. If Dad is involved, this is a time to explain how Asperger people and others communicate very differently. Estelle and I have discovered this act of interpretation has done a lot for Jared, and also our marriage. It is important for Jared to know his parents support each other. But, it is equally wonderful to have your spouse support you, knowing they will not agree with negative talk about you.

Living out well-defined roles has helped Jared to know what to expect from Estelle and me. I take opportunities to model and teach Jared what a man is. As different situations arise, I ask him one of my standard questions, "What would a man do?" When he was younger, I told him what a man would do. Now I let him make that decision and tell me what a man would do. It really helps Jared learn decision-making skills and evaluate his own value system. Jared is my student in all areas of life. I often approach tasks, situations, and decisions with Jared as a teaching opportunity.

Estelle plays a key role in keeping the stress level down in our home. We have come to realize that the lady of the house sets the emotional climate. When Estelle is happy, nothing seems that bad. When she is upset, minor issues appear bigger than what they really are. Estelle uses this emotional advantage to help Jared recover from conflict with Dad. When a disagreement leaves Jared pretty upset or angry, Estelle will stay removed from the situation. She simply acts as cheery and positive as possible. This takes a hard situation with a heavy atmosphere in the home and turns it into a lighter, or happier climate again. Keeping the emotional tone more level allows me to be more rational. Stress is a major distraction in interpersonal relationships and often decision-making.

Communication is clearly a critical skill for parenting in our Asperger family. Estelle often sees things softer, whereby I see things clearer. Estelle senses the emotions and heart attitude involved in interpersonal situations. She also somehow feels it to some degree. This affects the clearness of her viewpoint, but also allows her to interpret and be a "cookie giver" later. On the other hand, I "read" all the criteria available. I look at facts and face the truth of the matter in a detached sort of way. This gives me a "clear" picture.

By combining these two viewpoints, Estelle and I better decide what and how to deal with Jared. Simply recognizing and verbalizing the way we come to our viewpoints helps us communicate better with each other. If we anticipate disciplining Jared for a greater offense, we collect all the facts we can, including from Jared. We talk privately, get in agreement, and then we get Jared involved. Estelle and I try to allow Jared to walk us through his offense as well as his thoughts at the time. We also allow him to see the effect it has on us. Oftentimes this brings the situation to a relational level.

Because I sometimes get on a roll of listing details and facts concerning the "crime" committed, Estelle often helps break my pattern. She will inform me that I am going on too much or being too mechanical and detailed. She will then explain or interpret how she thinks Jared is feeling and what he is thinking. This is helpful as oftentimes, I am clueless as to what he is thinking. I think I know, so I believe a lecture is the answer. Then I find out I am way out in left field. By letting Estelle communicate her thoughts on the matter, I am preventing myself from being unfair and creating deep anger in Jared.

Using family rules and guidelines helps to keep order in our home. Giving Jared a vision, using interpretation skills, living out well-defined roles as parents, and adequate communication are key tools that Estelle and I practice while raising our son. This foundation provides for a healthy family and an enjoyable marriage.

8

Professional and Personal Relationships as Seen by Friends and Co-workers

Writing this chapter was really insightful! We gained some valuable information from some of our long-time friends and some of Patrick's co-workers, who allowed me to spend time interviewing them. Now, knowing the cause for Patrick's unique eccentricities, we are becoming more comfortable with sharing the world of Asperger Syndrome (AS) with others. However, none of the individuals whose personal insight is included in this chapter had any prior knowledge of AS while going into a relationship with Patrick. Each chose to make a conscious decision, at one time or another, to understand his inner workings. What makes him tick? How does he function? What will my relationship be with him?

Because an outsider's view allows for a fuller picture of the world touched by Asperger Syndrome, we are grateful for our friends agreeing to help us broaden the scope of this book. Paul's view (though also a friend) comes from his position as an agricultural supervisor, responsible to

Patrick at the rescue mission where he is currently employed. Traci speaks as Paul's wife and an observer of the rescue mission work. Lenina's insight is from time spent working with Patrick for the Department of Justice. Bill, Jean, Ramon and Jillian, (family friends and one-time neighbors), Bryan and Kristin (friends who also worked for Patrick) also gave valuable contributions to the creation of this chapter. The hope of each of these individuals, as well as ourselves, is for others to benefit by the experience and details shared.

Before going any further, it is important to understand some facts about *how* a person with AS learns to relate with others. The social skill of relating is a learned process of reading, analyzing and observing. Since one of Patrick's special interests is the study of people, I have bestowed upon him an honorary doctorate degree in the study of humanity. Every person he comes in contact with is immediately placed under a microscope for the express purpose of understanding the human race. Every detail of every person comes under an intense scrutiny.

Kristin thinks this special interest of Patrick's is fascinating. She enjoys Patrick's hobby of people watching and has great fun watching him watch others! Whenever our two families spend time together, Kristin is quick to get Patrick's analysis of those around us. While eating a meal together during our last visit, Kristin sat back with a big smile on her face and began to ask Patrick questions to put his people watching/analysis skills to work! Bryan also sees Patrick's valuable insight, "due to his unique ability to analyze deeply, drawing accurate information on the character of others."

Paul and Traci both feel that this type of learning can perpetuate over-analysis. Patrick reads body language, trying to understand what a person is thinking. Since body language is different from one person to the next, Paul feels that people can be misinterpreted at times. However, most of the time Patrick's analysis is correct.

Another result of over-analysis Paul shared is that at times Patrick believes there is a relational issue between Paul and himself. The reality is that there's an issue, but it is not a relational one. Paul shared an example of when this sometimes happens. When Paul has structure, work goes well and much is accomplished. At that point, he begins to invest more time interacting with the rescue mission residents on a personal level. But then he falls behind in his work and has difficulty catching up. When this happens, Patrick sometimes thinks there is a relational issue between Paul and himself. In reality, more often than not, Paul is actually struggling with his priorities being out of balance.

People with AS have a unique way of relating to others, one of which occurs in communication. Our friends find that conversations with Patrick appear devoid of emotion. During these interactions, they feel that what is being communicated is without meaning. A friend may not feel the words communicated, even when Patrick is speaking words of love and affirmation. Words seem to be spoken at them, not to them. Traci finds Patrick to be quite knowledgeable on the proper way of relating to others, making great effort to follow the social norms of communication. But since he is not emotionally attached to a conversation, Patrick's communication tends to be blunt or harsh due to his brutal honesty and straightforwardness. Jillian gave an example of Patrick's seeming harshness when giving her some marital advice. He just said what needed to be said. Without a hint of feeling in his voice, he said something like, "Well, Jillian, you should not say thus and so to your husband." Jillian felt this quite brutal. But because she had great respect for him, she accepted his words as from his heart. She relayed that though Patrick may have cushioned the interaction with words of love and emotion, the cushion was not *felt*.

Jillian's view on the topic of bluntness in a conversation is that each culture has its own way of communicating, with Americans tending to cushion what we want to say. In a conversation in which truth needs to be spoken, generally, we use a sandwich affect saying the necessary words between words of affirmation, a compliment or encouragement. Jillian says that Patrick has made an intellectual identification of tactful ways of relating to people. She knows he has purposed in his heart to communicate in a way others can accept. However, even though his words follow the pattern of what is normal, since the feelings aren't communicated as well, they are not heard. Though he tries hard, he cannot change the flat communication, which has a negative effect on many relationships.

Jillian feels that non-Asperger communication is based on feelings. When faced with a situation in which someone might be offended by what we say, the situation is entered into with apprehension. The feelings of others are dealt with in response to the emotion in the situation. Jillian sees that AS people respond on a different level in the same situation than do others.

Lenina's insight into Patrick's brutal honesty is that Patrick didn't develop the other "self" who can say the words people want to hear. Lenina shares that she has a new understanding of this straightforwardness since her not too distant motor vehicle accident. She feels she no longer has the tolerance to say what people want to hear or to kowtow to their social expectations. Lenina believes that part of her initial frustration with Patrick was her being used to others' lack of truthfulness and straightforwardness. People would not say what needed to be said due to their fear of appearing impolite.

In dealing with Lenina, Patrick would simply state the truth of a matter. He would state the obvious, what everyone knew to be true, but feared having it brought out into the open. Lenina shared a humorous example of how Patrick would handle her having a purple face as compared to a normal complexion. Patrick would say, "Lenina, you have a purple face. How interesting!" And for so many years the whole world would have known about her purple face but never said anything to her about it. Lenina said she has learned to appreciate this honest communication knowing that a good friend is genuine and truthful.

Many possible friendships with Asperger people never occur because of misunderstandings in the initial flat conversation. During the first handshake, it seems that people tend to investigate the possibility of a relationship with each other. Patrick, appearing to be devoid of emotions, is a deterrent in that situation. He often is not afforded a second chance with new acquaintances. His affect is flat emotionally, so people frequently are apprehensive, tending to avoid the different individual after the initial meeting.

Lack of connecting emotionally seems to be another difficulty in communication. It seems especially true with women, that if Patrick does not connect with them emotionally the first time, they will avoid him. They do not understand, so they avoid what they do not understand. This can be very painful, as Patrick only desires what's best for them.

When first getting to know Bill and Jean, I invited their whole family over for a meal. Jean remembers being uneasy with Patrick because he seemed so solemn and stern. She kept hoping that the kids wouldn't do anything to upset him. Jean shared the contrast between Patrick and myself. As I am very approachable, with a bubbly and inviting personality, Jean says that she can relate to me easily. However, Jean finds difficulty in knowing what Patrick is thinking. After getting to know him, Jean has come to realize "he's just that way." But, until then, she always felt as if he was mad and was intimidated by him.

Jean also found one-on-one conversation with Patrick to be challenging and insightful. He never asked questions that would create embarrassment, but rather conducted conversations like an interview. Jean concluded that since Patrick enjoys deep issues rather than just chit chatting, one would be wise to think before answering his questions!

Another difficulty in relating with others comes in the form of confusion and frustration. When Lenina first began working with Patrick, she didn't like him and her impression of him was negative. He was confusing and she often was frustrated with her inability to understand him. He spoke in a realm which was difficult to comprehend. She then found that he was extremely intelligent, therefore having a hard time coming down to our level to communicate in a way we can understand. Because of this, Lenina believes that AS people are easily misunderstood. Eventually, she found Patrick to be reliable, having knowledge, integrity and someone she could trust. Lenina's confusion from her initial conversations was on a personal level, but she didn't allow that to hinder her desire to work with him.

Paul brought up another important factor in relating; the *thinking* of Asperger people is different than others. Their thinking is objective, not emotional. Paul says that this is important to understand when sharing something emotional with a person who thinks objectively. The discussion must be objective rather than emotional. So Paul explains that if there is an offense needing to be aired, one should think through it before talking about it. How can this be communicated in a way that will be understood? Simply dumping emotion onto the objective Asperger individual will not attain the desired outcome.

Patrick interprets the importance of what Paul is saying in the following way. "The person with Asperger Syndrome has only good intent. However, their delivery in conversation is often unusual and unnerving, which can be misunderstood. Or, they do something that creates irritation. At this point, they desire for people to simply talk to them about the problem, but not to raise their voice in anger and frustration. The AS individual is affected to a greater degree by the raised voice and intensity of others than a 'normal' person; it is greatly magnified, so they feel it more. Talking objectively to the person with Asperger Syndrome will get a serious response. The AS individual *wants* to explain, but simply desires for others to be gentle and kind in dealing with them."

Although members of the Asperger world think objectively, they still do have emotions. Jillian believes that though Patrick does not feel that much of what he does is different, he does comprehend the difference. Being able to see the great effort Patrick makes in relating with others helped her in committing to him as a friend. Jillian believes that he has great remorse at times because he cannot function as others need him to. She sees Patrick as knowing he is not capable of being "normal," but accepting this as something he cannot change.

Because I am able to read Patrick's emotions better than others, I am well aware that great agony is often felt by his over-analysis of situations beyond his control. When a "normal" individual messes up, he may feel badly but move on. Patrick, however, will go to an extreme in feeling badly about his mistake, especially when it affects others. He will find great difficulty letting go of these negative emotions.

Because, in relating to others, AS people do not show their emotions in the same manner as others do, some think they don't have emotions. This false thinking results in the Asperger individual being treated as one who cannot be hurt emotionally. In reality, people with AS seem to be more sensitive to emotions and the spoken word of others. Because Patrick speaks exactly what he means, the careless words of another are accepted as from the heart. One may never see the unintended harm that they cause, but loved ones will quickly take note of the retreat to the safety zone.

An example of an event, which has left Patrick reeling with emotional pain, happened a while ago. He was filling in as executive director for a regional rescue mission. Patrick was in a conversation with a husband and wife, who were new to rescue mission work, along with another volunteer. The husband asked Patrick about one of the residents who was threatening to leave the mission. Patrick responded with common rescue mission philosophy, which was not well received by the wife. As Patrick could tell she did not like his words (due to the angry look on her face), he attempted to help her with emotion and logic. "I hope this doesn't upset you," Patrick communicated with genuine care and concern. "In rescue mission work, you will understand that sometimes people just aren't ready for long-term help." But, instead of hearing his words, she emoted her feelings with, "That's okay. You'll be gone in two weeks and someone else will be here who thinks differently!"

Patrick again tried to explain that the opinion he voiced was not his own; he had learned this philosophy from his co-workers and experience in rescue mission work, but she abruptly turned away leaving the other three in an awkward position. The woman's husband and other volunteer, seeing what just took place, felt terrible and tried to compensate for her behavior. However, even with their condolences this incident continues to hurt Patrick to this day. Her emotional outburst and rejection of him on a personal level (due to his voicing a rescue mission truth) is still felt by him.

Body language is another way in which people with AS seem to feel the intensity of our emotions. Body language shows a great deal of emotion when one is anxious or excited. Patrick once described my behavior as "shaking back and forth, staring straight ahead, holding your body all rigid, and waving your arms." This behavior is very bothersome because the AS person feels as if the other person is losing control of himself. Patrick says, "This behavior is completely unnecessary, reaching the point of unpredictability and confusion." He sees this as "unsettling, creating anxiety and irritability, *especially* because it is unnecessary." Patrick says, "The showing of irritation, aggravation and aggression through body language leads to emotions controlling the situation, rather than common sense and logic controlling the situation. This then leads to unpredictability, which leads to the probability of a change in mood and structure of the home, workplace, and relationships." Patrick feels that this behavior is unnecessary; to simply talk and sort out the situation is a better way of handling it.

Emotions of concern, understanding, and protectiveness were seen in Patrick when Lenina worked in a prison for the Department of Justice. Lenina was involved in an emergency situation when Patrick responded to her call for help. Even though Lenina freezes (instead of screams) when becoming scared, Patrick could tell that she was shaken. Lenina shares that Patrick's calmness and ability lent an element of normalcy and stability to an intense situation. This incident convinced her that out of all the people working in the prison, Patrick was the one she wanted to work with.

Receiving verbal feedback is another indication of the emotions alive in the Asperger individual. Paul sees Patrick's desire to be in right relationship with his co-workers as a noticeable quality. Although this is common with many people, it is the *way* Patrick seeks feedback, when unsure of where he stands with others, that Paul had to get used to. Paul says that it is not every day that a man will approach another man and ask, "Have I done something to offend you?" Patrick does what he can to ensure all of his relationships are in good standing.

Relating with others in the workplace has its differences as well. Paul's insight is that some feel insecure around Patrick due to his intensity level and self-confidence. Patrick quickly learns the inter-working of every area of his work environment. This tremendous knowledge of every employee's responsibilities makes others feel insecure. But, Patrick has no desire for his co-workers to experience insecurity; he's not even aware of this taking place. Paul sees that when Patrick's co-workers decide to focus on his heart (instead of his actions), they soon realize that his only desire is to be helpful. Those who choose this route of seeing Patrick as a person with a different way of relating, are more likely to listen, accept advice, and become better for the experience.

The way an Asperger individual relates to others with humor and fun is also unique. In the workplace, Patrick feels that new staff initially perceive him as a focused, driven, "type A" person who has no time for enjoying life. Though he finds many of their jokes funny, he doesn't think they are funny enough to laugh at. This can create major problems because people sometimes view this as a personal offense. Patrick knows that humor is needed in the workplace and wants to join in the fun. However, new staff are slow to realize Patrick is friendly, congenial and desires to enjoy them, not just work with them. This can make working with new staff very difficult and unpleasant for months, unless other staff, who understand Patrick, interpret him to them.

Patrick's friends realize that his standards of relaxing and having fun are just different. Patrick *is* intense, they say, and it is hard for him to have fun and let his hair down, so to speak. Jean describes times of lightheartedness when, "Patrick would be quite serious. All of us would be cutting up and having a good time, but Patrick would still be solemn or stern." He was not necessarily having a bad time, just being himself.

In the workplace, Paul finds that Patrick really struggles with having fun. His conclusion is that it is really hard for a person with AS to have fun *with* people. Paul also finds the types of activities Patrick enjoys quite amusing. He thinks that Patrick's enjoyment of Morse code, his sense of humor, and his hobby of studying people are all unique ways of enjoying life! Paul has come to believe that Patrick takes great joy in his work of managing well!

To Patrick, work can be pleasurable, and pleasurable situations, he makes more like work. For those who want to share pleasure with their Asperger friend, this is a bit difficult. In any activity he involves himself in, Patrick will totally focus. Bill remembers bringing two motorcycles over to our house. He enjoyed watching Patrick's excitement as a huge grin spread across his face. A pleasurable experience, he didn't skip a beat in getting the bikes fixed up.

As Patrick rolled the motorcycle off of the truck and around to the back of our tiny apartment at language school, the temperature was well into 120 degrees fahrenheit. Bill was trying to get Patrick inside to wait for a better time, but Patrick was totally focused. Bringing out his heavy toolboxes, he called for Jared to assist him. With sweat dripping down his glasses and blurring his vision, he wouldn't quit. His mission was not complete until the motors were running and they took them for a ride. Patrick would wear himself out before quitting. As most people tend to separate work and play, enjoying life with their Asperger friend can be a difficult task.

Anti-social behavior and the need for purposeful withdrawal at times are also unique aspects affecting relationships between AS people and the outside world. Patrick's friends think it beneficial to have an interpreter to make sense of this behavior. Without this interpretation, Jillian is certain that people with Asperger Syndrome are lost to the world. She feels that others would not understand Patrick and therefore would avoid him.

Jillian and I enjoyed a good laugh when remembering an example of Patrick's anti-social behavior. While living together in a closed community as language students, Jillian often would come to visit after being certain we were home. She knocked at the back door, but got no response. Thinking we may not have heard the knock, Jillian walked around to the front of the apartment building to knock at the front door. Passing by the closed curtains in the front window, she peered into the living room where she could see the top of Patrick's head in his favorite chair. Being persistent, she began knocking at the front door and again there was no movement inside. Jillian was very frustrated, as she did not understand why Patrick was responding to her this way.

This form of relating was much different than what she was accustomed to. Jillian understood that there are times when people screen calls or don't answer their door, but knows that it is considered very rude to behave in this fashion when others *know* you are home. When I interpreted on Patrick's behalf, Jillian was able to see that, though Patrick was clearly being anti-social, his behavior toward her was not personal. This helped her to gain clarity of the situation and understand him better. Jillian was able to accept that Patrick was simply not ready for company and needed to withdraw socially.

Another example of Patrick's anti-social behavior is his unwillingness to talk on the phone. Since moving away, a few years have passed without Patrick speaking with Ramon and Jillian. So when we ladies were conversing, I tried to get Patrick to speak with Jillian on the telephone. Patrick's response was, "You know I hate to talk on the phone," while accepting the phone from me. A typical reaction from most people would be to have hurt feelings, thinking Patrick as rude. Jillian, understanding Patrick's anti-social behavior and knowing his intent was not malicious, spoke to him with kindness. And, in return, she says she was blessed with such kind words, "like a beautiful gift." Jillian finds this behavior quite fascinating! Equally amazing to Jillian is, "When Patrick is forced (by social constraints) to talk on the phone, he does not respond in the same way as others do. Instead of being non-communicative, he has very meaningful substantial conversations. When he puts his mind to it, Patrick does not struggle with engaging in thoughtful, deep, intense, and incredible encounters with the outside world."

Those who know Patrick say that more commitment is required (from both parties) in their relationship with Patrick than in other relationships they are involved in. Having to commit on a deep level relationally, however, is scary for some people. Jillian, however, did not struggle with her commitment to a relationship with Patrick. She saw his depth of commitment to her. And when Bryan saw the value of a friendship with Patrick, along with his commitment, he also became willing to make the depth of commitment required. The non-AS person must be willing to be extra committed and faithful to the relationship if he wants to befriend his AS acquaintance. So, having a relationship with an AS person is harder since both individuals need to be more accepting of each other's differences.

Paul shared some additional insight on the commitment level of AS people. He says that Patrick has a tendency to believe that others share the same level of commitment as he does. When Patrick's non-AS friend does not show the same depth of concern for him as he has for his friend, it means he does not care. Although this is not true, it seems difficult for Patrick to comprehend. Paul says that he has learned the importance of honoring his commitments to Patrick. When he doesn't, Patrick assumes that either something seriously went wrong, or that Paul does not care about the relationship. Paul believes that honoring commitments is valuable in all relationships, but since an AS person trusts you, he will hold you accountable. This was a huge concept for Paul to understand.

Patrick's loyalty and integrity is seen in his relationships with his friends and co-workers. Bill shared an example of Patrick's loyalty to him when we were moving away from Texas. After the trailers were loaded up with all of our belongings and the vehicles ready to leave, Patrick stopped by Bill's house to ask if there was anything else he could do for him before leaving the state. Bill, with a grin ear-to-ear and ready for some fun said, "When you get to Yellowstone, pick up a buffalo chip for me!" Patrick cocked his head to one side in wonder at the request. Then, when he believed Bill to be sincere, agreed to the wild idea. As our family headed north, I immediately forgot about Bill's special package. And I bet Bill didn't think much about it either until receiving his chip in the mail, along with a photo to prove its owner a certifiable American bison! But Patrick, true to his word, did not rest until his mission was complete. Bill recalled the incident to me later and said that when he opened his package, he just imagined Patrick not sleeping until he boxed up that chip and dropped it off at the post office!

Having Patrick as his boss, Paul appreciates his moral code of ethics. Paul has discovered Patrick to be very loyal and committed to honesty, regardless of his personal cost. Paul says, that "Even if Patrick dies in the process, he *will* keep his word." As a subordinate, Paul finds security in knowing that his boss will back him up. When Patrick believes in what his employees are involved with, they will find him quite supportive.

Even in the workplace, Patrick strives to avoid bothering or offending his co-workers. Paul's example of this attribute was when he shared with Patrick that a word he commonly used really offended him. Since that time, Paul states that Patrick has never again used it in his presence. On occasion, after realizing Paul was within earshot when Patrick used the offensive word, he was quick to apologize.

Another factor Bryan feels that a friend of an Asperger person needs to understand is his/her tremendous need for structure. An average person doesn't struggle much with a change in plans, but the person with AS struggles with adapting to sudden change. These changes are significant for Patrick to deal with. Bryan learned to plan activities in advance instead of just showing up at our house with suggestions on places to go or things to do.

While still getting to know Patrick, Bryan really wondered if Patrick's structure was created as a desire to present a certain image or if it was a genuine part of his personhood. To test out his theory, Bryan switched a stapler and tape dispenser on Patrick's desk without Patrick's knowledge. (I have since been informed that Patrick currently has co-workers moving items around on his desk to see what he will do! They have no knowledge of Patrick's extreme need for order.) Patrick returned to his office and began talking to Bryan, calmly placing each item in their correct positions on the desk without a second thought. Bryan was quite amazed and quickly became a believer in Patrick's deeply ingrained need for structure.

Kristin also believed initially that Patrick was just being picky and demanding that everything be his way or not at all. She recalled a time, before having a name for the face of AS, when I used to return money to Patrick's wallet. Later, as Patrick got into his wallet, we would all watch as he "freaked out" finding the disarray. Each bill had a precise place of its own and a precise way to exist. The small denominations went in the front going in order with the larger denominations in the back. Kristin also noticed how Patrick would quietly abstain from eating when food was not made the usual way. She began to understand that he had no choice, that deep inside of Patrick there is a *need* for structure and order.

At the rescue mission, Paul observes that having structure is vital to a smooth environment. Paul says that the more structure Patrick has, the more he is able to accomplish. His mind is free to plan and deal with deeper issues in life, rather than just the day-to-day issues. But, when there is a lack of structure, Patrick's day is ruined. His energy is then focused on simply trying to re-structure the day. As this happens, Paul sees that Patrick loses flexibility, becoming increasingly difficult to work with.

Living the structure out, Patrick accomplishes more than others, yet sometimes he misses opportunities for connecting on the emotional level. At this point, Paul advises that co-workers should understand that if structured time is not available, they should wait until later for discussion with Patrick. Traci feels that people should not be upset with Patrick for this, but instead be understanding that this is how he needs to function. When able, Patrick will drop everything and be quite flexible, especially when others need his help.

Paul's view of the environment created by Patrick's structure is one of more peace, less stress and much easier in which to work. Before Patrick structured the workplace, using a myriad of schedules, reports and forms, the rescue mission had many crises and was a pandemonium. Initially, employees did not welcome the newly structured environment, but instead reacted as if this new operations manager was simply a control freak. Now, however, Traci points out that the structure has made the ministry more successful. She sees that people are communicating with one another and there is more understanding between the staff members as well as the residents.

An additional consideration Bryan mentioned in relating to a person with AS is the need for a friend to be strong. Bryan sees that this will give balance to the relationship. Patrick easily plans out activities, having the best ideas and methods to engage the activity, but Bryan's feeling is that this is one-sided. He says that friends need to provide balance by initiating activities, giving their ideas, and sometimes questioning what the Asperger friend wants to do. To Bryan, it is apparent that the one with AS tends toward extremes in everything he endeavors to do, because he does it with all of his heart. But, sometimes just dabbling into a hobby or activity, rather than submerging yourself into it is better. Patrick is an all or nothing kind of guy, but sometimes, partial commitment is required.

Bryan brought up an example of how he dealt with Patrick's tendency toward extremes when our families were visiting together. Patrick communicated that he had an important issue to discuss with us all. When the little kids were tucked into bed and Jared was out with a friend, Patrick became very serious as he discussed a topic of importance to him. There was tenseness in the air as Patrick asked each of us to make a lifetime commitment involving our future. Bryan gave pause to that, as he was not ready to make that kind of commitment. In his opinion, this same discussion with another friend would require less commitment. Bryan says that others might still make a commitment they cannot keep due to their feeling pressured. But Bryan feels that his being a strong person gives balance to his relationship with Patrick.

Those who spend much time with Asperger individuals quickly realize the great desire they have to share their abundant knowledge with others. Patrick says, "We want to share our knowledge so others can have the same benefit that we gain from it." Lenina realized one of the advantages of working with Patrick was his immense knowledge of all the rules. Whenever she had any doubt about what regulation affected a given situation, she would ask Patrick and, "He would spout out all of the information just like a dictionary!"

Jean appreciated Patrick's knowledge in a class we took together as couples. Since Patrick enjoys facts and studying, he always had valuable insight to offer the class. Jean felt that Patrick's presence demanded for the instructor to really know the information he was presenting. Though not pushy, Patrick was quick to correct an untruth, which caused for a more interesting experience!

But Paul cautions that in the workplace, Patrick's sharing of personal insight can sometimes be dangerous in the wrong hands. Paul realizes that Patrick is just trying to give him insight on how to view others. When Patrick discusses co-workers, he is not trying to badmouth them, just stating reality. But Traci sees that since Patrick has no emotional connection with the facts discussed, he does not comprehend how his actions can be so traumatic for the individual involved. Since Patrick has no desire to hurt others, he does not understand the negative emotional reactions others have as a result of his sharing personal observations of them.

Paul shares the importance of communication in the workplace. This is helpful as people with AS desire to get along with others, especially in the workplace. In order to do this, they need *ample* communication, as well as a greater *depth* of communication. Communication is what holds all things together, so more time may be spent in communication with an AS boss than with a boss not having Asperger Syndrome. Paul believes it extremely important that Patrick's subordinates view the extra communication as a protection, not an intrusion. Patrick has no desire to be controlling, but instead wants to support his employees. Paul sees that it is crucial to find a means of communication that is effective for both the boss and employee. As Paul has worked in agriculture most of his life, he had been used to communicating during a meal shared together with his co-workers. But, upon coming to work for Patrick, he had to change his style of communication. He tried various means of communication, before finding an effective style. For Paul, the email system works well for him, though he believes that daily communication in person is Patrick's preferred method.

Traci complemented this discussion with how communication affects relationships. She sees that communication for Patrick can be extremely frustrating, since he wants to fully understand what is being communicated to him. Because Patrick tries very hard to understand, when the words of others don't make sense, he becomes very frustrated. Traci explains that when Patrick struggles to understand on the emotional level, he has a need to know the intimate details of a situation, but the individual himself may not even know those details.

Another difference in communication is what I call the "truth factor." It seems that a regular friendship includes the hope of truthfulness, without the expectation of truthfulness. For Patrick, the telling of white lies and other lies immediately ends the relationship. Whether the relationship is with a possible friend or co-worker, a lack of truthfulness destroys any kind of friendship that might have otherwise occurred.

One characteristic attributed to AS which appears to especially affect Patrick's work relationships is his extreme attention to details. Paul shares that his boss reads and files every report written, which may be helpful if the information documented would ever be needed. However, some employees can be quite insecure with this attention to detail, since Patrick holds them to their word. This isn't a problem for Paul as his reports are honest and he has nothing to hide.

Patrick also *sees* the report in more detail than others do and makes ample comments regarding each report. Since Patrick checks his subordinates' work very closely, employees may not feel trusted. Paul stresses the need for employees not to take having their work being cut to shreds (by their detail-oriented boss) personally. Patrick only desires for his personnel to strive for a higher level of work performance. Paul also shares another way he's learned to deal with Patrick's attention to detail, to always turn work in early. This ensures he will have plenty of time for corrections!

Though Patrick is extremely detailed, at times he only wants simplicity. Paul shares an amusing situation that happened recently. He had worked hard to supply his boss with a very detailed agricultural report/forecast. He felt pleased with his work, confident that Patrick would be happy with it. But much to his surprise, he received a call from Patrick asking, "Paul, could you make this more simple? We don't need all the details." Was he hearing correctly? This was not the Patrick he had grown to understand! He was quite shocked and bewildered! What Paul didn't know was that the management team from headquarters couldn't understand the massive amounts of detail and agricultural terminology. They were having detail overload! Though the report was wonderful to Patrick, with all details fine-tuned, it was confusing the ones who had requested the information.

To the AS manager, attention to detail in work area cleanliness shows how well you are performing. To Patrick, a tidy work area represents the high quality of work being accomplished. If a person does not take the time for the details of cleanliness, he also must not care about what he is doing. Paul suggests that new employees should walk through their work area together with their boss. Paul has found that has helped him to see the work environment as Patrick sees it, while at the same time provided him with lots of work to accomplish! Paul advises not to make the same mistake that he did by only having one sheet of notebook paper to write on! Quickly running out of paper, he found that even a rock was out of place! But, until Paul spent time walking through his work area with Patrick, he had no idea of the disarray which was a glaring eyesore to his boss! As a result of this simple effort, Paul now has gained an eye for details.

Well-maintained files on each employee are another tribute to Patrick's attention to detail that Paul finds amazing. Patrick frequently adds notes to these files, using information recorded to give valuable insight during the employee's yearly review. As Paul states, since yearly reviews are opportunities to analyze an employee's work performance, bosses usually want to discuss ways to improve. Though Patrick is quick to remind each employee of their positive achievements, hearing lots of negative details at once can be quite crushing! Paul stresses the need for employees to understand why Patrick does this, so they won't feel so demoralized.

Patrick, always desirous of learning more details, will ask his employees to teach him anything he doesn't already know about their jobs. Paul finds this difficult to do in that agriculture does not follow a formula; the details of agriculture have too many variables. Since agriculture is not like a machine which only functions one way, Paul finds it difficult to teach Patrick the details he is so ready to learn.

All of our friends interviewed strongly concur that a person with AS is benefited greatly by having a non-Asperger spouse. Jillian's insight is that a non-AS spouse is a grounding point, giving the Asperger person feedback into others' lives and minds. She saw Patrick and I communicating a great deal. Jillian believes that a spouse can be a buffer between the world and the AS person. Bryan's view is that balance can be provided in a marriage in the same way that a friend can provide balance to the relationship. A non-AS spouse can help balance out the level of intensity with which his/her Asperger partner goes into a relationship or a project. Bryan sees my interpreting as helpful in understanding where others are coming from. Without the interpretation, Bryan says, an AS individual might take offense by someone who didn't mean to offend; that person simply may not have understood his expectations. Or, the non-AS friend may be offended by something the AS friend said or did.

For Patrick, the interpretation I do relieves a lot of stress and confusion. He says that my interpretation prevents him from closing off relationships he otherwise would have shut off. Jillian fears that without a "buffer," AS people would isolate themselves. She is bothered by the amount of isolation another AS acquaintance we both know experiences and laments his having to experience this loneliness. Lenina believes that our relationship helped her to understand Patrick, even though we did not yet have a name to the face of AS. She found my interpretation of Patrick the key to her acceptance of his unique behavior.

One difficulty in a marriage between an AS spouse and a non-AS spouse, however, is the communication factor. Both Patrick and I have to work very hard to understand each other. As Kristin said, "Interpretation for others can take place, but who is going to interpret for both of you?" Patrick brought up another difficulty for the Asperger individual married to the non-AS person. He continually tries adjusting to doing things on the spur of the moment, or having to answer to questions about "how he *feels* about things." The "normal" spouse frequently changes plans after decisions are already made and this is very hard and stressful.

Bryan and Kristin shared the importance of the need for structure. Their advice to the non-AS spouse is, "to be patient and understanding, assisting in creating order and structure, not to fight, but to comply." Jillian also noticed the extremely strict guidelines and structure within our home, even in unstructured modes. Jillian's advice for a spouse of an AS individual is, "to educate oneself and follow through with commitments and love."

In general, since in Patrick's opinion, "People are extreme variables, unpredictable, and often not very interested in relationships that require effort," it seems that it would be easier for an AS man to be married to an AS woman. But Patrick advises "to simply talk calmly to your AS spouse when trying to sort out any confusion, misunderstanding or frustration." Regardless of the energy required, true enjoyment and fulfillment in a "mixed" marriage can be found when both individuals realize the tremendous gem they have in their spouse.

It appears to me that a person with Asperger Syndrome is either a villain to those who haven't taken the time to get to know him, or a hero to those who have. Patrick is at the top of Bill's list of the ten most influential people affecting his life. Bill states, "Patrick is a leader, a real man, upfront and honest, a close and good friend. I see him as an incredible human being. I have never seen Patrick as a 'special needs' individual, but someone I wanted to get to know better from the moment I first met him. He is as honest as honest could be, yet gentle. Patrick always treated you with tremendous respect. It was clear that he was the leader in the home. When Patrick was teaching me and he had to correct me, he was gentle enough." Bill concluded with wishing he could spend more time with Patrick.

Bill also is impressed by Patrick's ability to make up his mind to do something. Bill shared an example of Patrick doing "a tremendous job in great adversity with only his own back and imagination." While living in south Texas, Patrick had purchased a four-wheel drive Ford Bronco. The truck needed to be painted, but Patrick wasn't willing to invest a lot of his money into it. So off he drove to Wal-mart, buying some cans of spray paint. He then began taping the Bronco to prepare it for the new paint job. When Bill came by to visit, there was Patrick, out in the driveway spray-painting the Bronco with a little can of spray-paint! Bill was a bit shocked, as he "had never seen anyone do anything like that before!" Patrick, with nothing but sweat equity and cans of spray paint was making something happen, simply by creativity and effort.

Ramon and Jillian also spoke of Patrick being someone they greatly admired. Ramon said, "What can I say? He's my hero. He helped me in a way that no one else could! That's it!" Jillian says that she is fortunate to have an Asperger friend. She says, "Compared to what I have gained from the relationship, my cost has been so little." She shared that her great respect for Patrick allowed her to accept his difficult words of counsel. Jillian really wanted me to understand that their marriage was saved by the time Patrick and I invested into their lives. Ramon and Jillian are now, "Following the example modeled out before us," as they both work with other young couples.

Though these three specifically called Patrick their hero, all interviewed acknowledge that much is to be gained from rubbing shoulders with the world of Asperger Syndrome. But Paul says, "Often opportunities are lost due to the obvious differences exhibited in their behavior." Paul advises people to hear the heart of the person with Asperger Syndrome. He says there is a need for communication within himself "to see what these special individuals have to offer and accept the opportunity for growth available when exposed to them." Paul says, "We need to ask the 'why questions' and seek to understand that person even more than you would another. Why doesn't *he* feel what I am saying? Why is he so structured? Why doesn't he understand what I am trying to say? Why is he so angry? Why is he watching me closely? Why is he so detailed?" He concludes that when having a boss with AS, if a person takes the time for internal communication, he will grow in ways not anticipated.

Before concluding this chapter, I need to stress the importance our friends see in encouraging, not only those interacting with AS individuals, but also the individual himself who may be struggling with this syndrome. He may not have the benefit of having a name for the face of this disorder and wonder why his social life is so difficult. He also may not have a support base from which to draw encouragement and feedback. This individual needs to realize the great contribution the world will gain by his engagement with it. Those with AS can share with the non-AS population their many positive attributes, gifts and talent. These individuals can be incredible, faithful employees. They are needed in situations requiring organization and problem solving. Though relating to the outside world comes at a great price (as the struggle and energy exerted to interact socially is immense), the world will be a better place for having been touched by them.

Traci says, "Patrick should be an encouragement to others with AS. Patrick is a testimony of how a person with AS can learn to encourage and support others even when they don't understand all the feelings 'normal' people go through. All is not lost, just because a person with AS doesn't understand. This doesn't mean they can't learn to communicate the deep love and support they have for others. They can learn to communicate emotionally to an emotional world."

In conclusion, much valuable insight was gained by interviewing family friends, neighbors and Patrick's co-workers. I believe that their practical advice will be helpful to many who interact with the Asperger world. When we, as a society learn to think differently, and accept those who don't follow the normal codes of behavior, much will be gained. The wonderful people from Planet Asperger will then be allowed to be a tremendous asset to friends, co-workers and the community as a whole!

9

Some Differences between Asperger People and Others

How to Understand "Normal" People

There are many obvious differences between Asperger people and so-called "normal" folk. Although some of these differences may apply to all people, in truth, they are more amplified or exaggerated in the lives of those with Asperger Syndrome. Many of these differences can cause Asperger individuals to be misunderstood. Some of these are: being too focused at times, having all their emotions viewed as anger or frustration when they're not, excessive need of time alone, going into monologues, being too frank, not being able to read other's emotions and expecting too much perfection from other people. In this chapter, some of these differences will be covered, along with possible explanations as to how a person with Asperger Syndrome should view others.

Asperger people often appear robotic. Sometimes they seem not to be able to feel. It is not that they don't feel, rather that their feelings are either desensitized or overly sensitized. For instance, Asperger individuals may need to be told that it is cold enough outside to warrant a jacket so they will not get sick. A reminder may be needed that if they do not drink enough water, they will get dehydrated which will cause a headache. It is not enough just to say that it is cold or hot. One must give their loved one the logic for what he or she is to do. An Asperger person might not be aware of a gaping cut in their hand until someone points out the blood making a mess.

When Patrick was a teenager, the vice principal followed a trail of blood down the hallway that led to his classroom. Patrick did not know that it was he that was hurt until everyone noticed the trail ending at his desk. He was then sent to the emergency room for stitches. More recently, Patrick began complaining of severe pain in his arm that could only be mildly subdued by morphine. He did not connect his pain with a three-wheeler crash he had had just days before. On the other hand, for an Asperger person getting bumped into even slightly, can be very upsetting. Small jolts sometimes cause major outbursts. Patrick needs a lot of personal space so that a slight brush against him does not create stress. When going for a walk, it is necessary to allow Patrick to walk in a straight line, at a consistent pace. The dogs, as well as the people, have to be kept at a distance from him to avoid unnecessary collisions.

People seem to notice the emotional difference in those with Asperger Syndrome quicker than anything else. Emotions seems to be absent, although they are present. Patrick has no mental filing system for emotions. Emotions are not naturally organized and it is quite confusing as to how one should respond to others. Navigating emotionally around normal people is very difficult to do. Without the proper tools to work with in this area, Asperger people simply must live with it. They must learn what is expected for each and every situation, then mimic as much as possible.

Most people have their feelings involved in their daily lives, whereas Asperger people have logic and performance. Asperger people may perform their duties well at work or home, yet appear to be cold or quiet. Because of their performance, they believe that this is seen as an action of love. However, performance is not enough for normal people who also want the Asperger person to feel. If this skill is not learned, others become hurt, angry or they avoid the person with Asperger Syndrome because he is too strange to be around. When an Asperger individual practises proper emotional skills, he shows his care and concern for others, allowing them to be more comfortable in their grief or happiness. Sometimes, this does not work well. For example, my son (in Chapter 4) told about an incident when he cut his finger. In this situation, Patrick did what he was taught to do. However, the lack of emotion in his dad really hurt Jared, which, in turn, really bothers Patrick. Events such as this one serve as motivation to work harder at understanding the emotional realm.

To an Asperger individual, choosing emotions is like having a choice of only one or two colors, but having different shades of those colors to choose from. If normal people are not rewarded with one of those emotions (or colors), they do not understand. The interpretation is that the one with Asperger Syndrome does not care or is only performing because he must. The other side of that situation is how Asperger people interpret the emotions of others in their actions, facial expressions, body posture, etc. Outside help is often needed to know what the response is in other people. When normal people do not react in basic, normal emotional patterns, there is confusion. Happy, sad, angry, or excited emotions are all pretty simple. But when a special gift is given and the recipient just looks at the giver for a second or two (which seems like an eternity), then shows a basic emotion, this reaction is quite perplexing. What did that pause mean? Are the feelings and facials faked to make one think they liked the gift? When something is not understood in relationships with others, this is quite unsettling. For someone with Asperger Syndrome, it is helpful to ask a trusted friend or loved one to interpret what they view as the reaction of another. Even though the interpretation may seem odd, this is better than not having a clue and being totally confused. Often normal people can better understand normal people.

Many people do not mind being slightly or occasionally disorganized. The confusing part is that to an Asperger individual others' disorganization seems to bother them. Words such as, "I'm sorry I'm late. I am so mad at myself for losing my keys" or "Someday I'll get this place organized" communicate that a person is uncomfortable with their disorganization. In truth, however, most normal people do not care to be organized any more than is absolutely necessary. This is an interesting perspective and is very helpful. Knowing this fact about normal people helps the Asperger individual to relax to some degree about disorganization in the people around them.

Many normal people are organized in a general sense while Asperger people are organized in a very specific way. Going into a variety of situations properly informed is a benefit to the Asperger mind. When something is organized at work or in a social situation, knowing ahead of time that it will seem unorganized enables the Asperger person to relax. If a person goes into the situation anticipating the confusion, it is easier to deal with. One can collect information on areas that must be known about ahead of time. For Asperger people, others need to be allowed to be themselves. The Asperger person must accept the disorganization of others. The normal people can be allowed to swirl about in their confusion, while the one with Asperger Syndrome will be able to relax.

The difference in the level of performance in a normal person versus an Asperger person is another issue that is important to understand. For Partick as an Asperger person, he needs to be involved with a minimum of two things at once. Most normal people are happy to do only one thing at a time. For example, some folks are perfectly content to simply eat breakfast, Patrick has to read or be listening to the news, while eating. Otherwise he feels he is wasting his time. As an Asperger individual, Patrick enjoys getting more than one thing done at a time. This situation explains why many normal people get stressed over multi-task issues. Even when planning fun events, individuals only want the responsibility of planning for one part. They plan and execute their part, but let others do the rest.

It is worth mentioning that sometimes Asperger individuals are considered lazy or non-productive. This conclusion is made due to not being able to consider the processes taking place in their minds. Frequently, these folks are willfully immobilized and prevented from taking action. The Asperger person takes in the big picture of a situation and categorizes it down into a manageable size. He, at the same time, is taking inventory on his opinions, experiences and overall sense about the many aspects of what it is he is sorting out. As this is whittled down he forms an order of how and if these events should happen. Then the decision is made as to whether or not he will do it. If so, he proceeds. If not, he will begin the process over again. Some things hamper a person from completing this process, such as lacking vital details needed, having a logical reason for going through with the action, having a value system of what is important to him (helping family, getting promoted, etc.) or lacking the confidence necessary to go through with the decision. If this process is rushed, there will be a high level of stress to deal with and it will take longer, not happen quicker.

This process is exactly what happened one sunny day in the Dominican Republic. Our friends had just arrived on the island, so our family was showing them around the closest city. It had been decided that we would walk around and locate stores where they could find items they would need in the future. Upon disembarking from our vehicles, everyone had collected what was needed and was ready for the journey. However, Patrick stood stock still by the car and would not move. He was unable to just walk around, and needed a specific plan to follow. This put a temporary damper on the mood as no one knew which shops were where and we had no map to guide us along. After Patrick came up with a structure he could follow, our little group started out. Each weekend also needs a definite plan to follow. It is not okay to just wait and see what the day will hold. A plan needs to be made and executed for peace to be had.

The perception of accomplishing is another note-worthy topic. Often normal people like to do nothing, but there is no room in the Asperger mind for that concept. In our home, we have an individual affectionately called "The White Tornado." This is a nickname Patrick has well earned for his constant high level of productivity (plus his desire for constant and complete cleanliness). Activities must be challenging, or he becomes easily bored. Even though Patrick performs an exhausting job as an operations and facilities manager for a rescue mission, he still is not satisfied. Patrick has written a manual, and given training at national level, for the mission. It is important for others to understand Patrick's need for this constant high level of performance, or they may feel threatened by what they consider competition. Part of meeting his need for challenges is his present work of writing this book. He also is currently studying a new culture and considering a Master's degree. Patrick has an insatiable desire to learn, achieve, and conquer. How can anyone be content in doing nothing?

This difference in the need for constant activity is vital to know since it can be draining on loved ones and sometimes quite unrealistic. For instance, when Patrick is sick, he doesn't seem to understand that he cannot keep up as before. As he continues to try to keep up his tremendous productivity, he becomes more and more frustrated. If I can alert him to his illness and how it affects him, I can often ward off a major explosion. Either as a result of, or as an instigator of the Asperger person's drive to get things done, normal people often misunderstand these individuals. Sometimes they are viewed as angry, frustrated, uptight or even worse, uncaring or unloving. Once an Asperger individual realizes this, changes can be made to keep relationships healthy. A distinct effort can be made to show appreciation of others. This is especially helpful in dealing with in-laws and co-workers.

Another area necessary for Asperger people to understand concerns visualization. Apparently, most people do not have a need to visualize what they are getting into before getting involved. This concept is very difficult to accept, but necessary to understand. Since an Asperger person thinks normal people need the details about a situation (as he does), he is quick to spend ample time in a conversation explaining them. To be informed that these details are not needed will keep the conversation from becoming boring and keep the attention of the participants involved.

One can see the differences in those with Asperger Syndrome from normal people. There are many areas; however, we have only discussed a few. Feeling, both emotionally and physically, was explored. Understanding what normal people need in the way of emotions and how Asperger people have to learn proper emotional responses is vital to relationships. The differences in our comfort levels of organization are important. Productivity and accomplishing is a driving force for the person with Asperger Syndrome. And understanding the lack of the visualization process in the mind of a normal person is also a valued insight.

10

A Look at Positive Aspects of Having Asperger Syndrome

This final chapter, looking at the positive aspects of having Asperger Syndrome, is intended to be informative, but even more importantly, encouraging. Although there are many positive attributes that accompany those with Asperger Syndrome such as, being observant, compassionate, having high IQs, being detailed, organized, analytical, task oriented, loyal, and having the ability to be rational and unemotional in a crisis, this chapter will only cover a few. Each of us will share our thoughts on this separately.

Jared's closing thoughts...

I would like to leave you with some lingering thoughts on a few of the positive aspects of Asperger Syndrome.

One of these is the fact that your AS parent is almost always more than willing to help you, and when he does, he does so until the target project is finished. He does this due to his need for completion, and desire to help. A recent example of this is when my dad helped me with my motorcycle tire. I have a Honda CB 750 motorcycle. My parents noticed just the other day that I have a nail in my back tire. I have needed a new tire for a while because my tread is going bald. (No, it is not because I have been doing burnouts.) Anyway, my dad decided to help me get a new tire. So the next day he called around to find the best tire price. He figured out a way to pay for it, and got it that day, all without my having to ask him for help, and all within about ten minutes. The morning after that, he helped me take my back tire off and put my bike on blocks. By myself this would have taken about four hours, but because of my dad's need for completion, and his desire to help, it only took about thirty minutes.

Another good quality is the AS parent's loyalty to their family and friends. In our world today, true loyalty is hard to come by. I recently had a neighbor back into my car. My dad was outside at the time, and I was inside doing something, so I did not hear the crunch. My dad quickly stopped the lady, and told her to wait until I could come and check it out. Somehow he found me and I went and looked to see how much of my car had been destroyed. Now someone else might have ran and told me that my neighbor had run into my car and that I need to come out and look. But he probably would not have stopped the lady in the car and made her get out and wait for me. Because of his loyalty to me and his ability to act well under pressure, both of which are Asperger traits, he did what he did.

One thing that has been really helpful to me is my dad's daily structuring of his time. Even though he does not have a cell phone or pager, I usually always know where he is and how to find him. This is nice because when I am out with my friends and I need to talk to him or ask for help, I can usually always get a hold of him.

In summary, there are many good things about Asperger Syndrome. However, I do not have nearly enough time or space to write about all of them. I have learned a lot in writing this, and I hope that in reading this book you will be helped greatly. The one thing that encompasses everything that I have written is this: communicate.

Patrick's closing thoughts...

It seems that there are positives and negatives to most things in life. Clearly, there are drawbacks to having Asperger Syndrome. I want to finish my part of this book thinking of the positives of what AS means in my life, particularly how it relates to people around me and what is required of me in life. This last chapter is a bit of a summary in a way. I'll be relatively brief and yet make my points. May these thoughts encourage you who read them.

Because I have a desire to observe what goes on around me and constantly learn new information and skills, I get a broad knowledge covering a variety of subjects. This is very handy. I can usually converse with anyone about whatever they want to. If I do not know about their subject of interest, I want to. I genuinely am interested in and ask about what they want to talk about. I get to learn more!

This broad base of interest or knowledge helps me get past my lacking social skills at times. My genuine interest in what others have to say keeps the door open with them, and prevents some relationships from ending at the first meeting. This trait also helps me when being asked to listen to others or give advice. I do care and usually have some understanding of their circumstances, either through my own life or that of others whom I have listened to. All this helps when giving feedback or simply directing others in coming up with their own solutions.

Being a detail-oriented guy comes in handy. It can lead to being too critical of others. I prefer to balance it out by using this trait to be helpful. Being aware of details helps me perform better at home and work. I don't believe I have ever forgotten a birthday, anniversary, or other significant days of Estelle's or Jared's! When I get my list of tasks to accomplish during my meetings with my supervisor, I make it complete. I follow through to the detail. My supervisors have appreciated this and have mentioned it several times over the years. This trait has helped balance out my performance evaluations at work as well.

Being one who stays calm during crises helps in several ways. I can often help things go smoothly and/or prevent the crisis from getting worse. This applies to an upset family member as well as a traffic accident, or other emergency.

My commitment level to those around me can be very beneficial to all concerned. I see my family, friends, and co-workers as people. I do not see them simply as an employee, wife, acquaintance, son, etc. Because of struggling to be understood at times, I strive to understand others. I try to sympathize or empathize with those around me. This allows me to better love them in thought, prayer, and deed. The traits I've mentioned in this section lend themselves toward being a better leader, lover, and supervisor. We all find ourselves in these positions at times.

I really enjoy my "special interests." When I think of people who do not practise a hobby or special interest, I feel sad for what they are missing. The joy and pleasure of studying people, motorcycling, reading, etc. is wonderful! I would be missing a great deal of pleasure in life if I didn't have my interests or hobbies outside of work and family.

While I love my family and friends, I can enjoy solitude. In fact, I really enjoy being alone. While some people need to be around people most of the time, I'd rather be alone most of the time. Solitude and silence are beautiful parts of life for me.

Estelle's closing thoughts…

Asperger traits and non-Asperger traits can both be viewed in either a positive or negative light. As I have shared in this book, I believe that a healthy support system is vital to the person with AS. People with Asperger Syndrome are no different than others in their need to be encouraged to grow in their gifts and abilities, and tone down their behavior which affects people in a negative way. When your AS loved one is valued for what s/he brings to a relationship in a positive way, this will help him/her to engage in life more often and in a deeper way.

One area frequently mentioned by other family members of AS individuals is their loved one's seeming lack of motivation. In Patrick's case, he is either "all on" or "all off." Patrick is either totally involved in a situation, or not involved at all. This may be misunderstood, but all who know Patrick well know he definitely does not suffer from a lack of motivation. What happens is that life must be organized. The tools and materials for the job must be available. The information for the situation needs to be understood. If these factors are not in place, then the AS individual cannot do what is expected.

An example of this is repairs or jobs around our house. Our family has been remodeling and fixing up a house we purchased close to three years ago. This means that we have had ample tasks to accomplish. Before we even signed the contract on the house, Patrick had a priority list in his mind of which jobs were to be done first, second and so on. However, each of these jobs was at a complete standstill until the money, time, and materials became available to complete the project. Once everything became available for each particular job then no time was wasted until the work was done. Leaving a job half finished is not an AS trait! What would take most individuals multiple days or hours to complete is finished in no time flat due to Patrick being "all on!" This is a very positive attribute to have in a husband when you want to have your house fixed up. ☺

Due to Patrick's intense study of life, he is extremely knowledgeable in many areas. Most people get an overall or general idea of specific areas of life, and a detailed knowledge in a few areas. But Patrick studies each area of life he comes in contact with to the greatest depth possible. Because of this, I can go to him for help with practically everything!

One area of life in which I have benefited by tapping into Patrick's knowledge is my employment. Since Patrick received a college degree in the management of human resources and continues to hone his skills in this area as a manager, he has great knowledge in this area. I have learned much about how to get along with others in the workplace, how to "dress for success," how to maintain a good reputation, how to be listened to when there is something the boss needs to know, and much more!

Another AS trait that I have modeled from Patrick is his great organizational skills. I have become very organized and detailed in my classroom at school. I have developed charts, forms, and other techniques to do my job well. Frequently, I get compliments on how organized I am! This has been a great benefit to my reputation as an employee.

Because I can learn about situations from Patrick before actually having to encounter them, I can gain confidence and experience life, as I never would have. One memory that comes to mind is our move to Hawaii. Patrick and I were a young military couple, newly married and moving to a place far from home. I knew no one, was unfamiliar with the island and didn't know how to drive our vehicle. Because Patrick had studied marriage and life in general, he knew that it was common for military wives to go into isolation, and therefore depression, when moving to a new home. No sooner had I arrived on the island than Patrick put me behind the wheel of our Volkswagen van. Having already explored, he showed me how to get to around the island to the places I would need to go and helped me to become familiar and unintimidated by the newness of it all. After I knew my way to the military base, the post office, and grocery store, he then worked on ways to get me connected with other military wives. I was able to really enjoy my time overseas while other wives were lonely and isolated in their homes.

Each of us has a choice to make in life, whether to look for the best in others or the worst. We can either build others up with our encouragement or tear them down with our criticism. I personally would like for others to accept me for who I am, while helping me to become a better person. As well, I should do the same for my husband with Asperger Syndrome.

Living and Loving with Asperger Syndrome is our family's life story. The purpose of exposing personal details of our lives is to somehow produce hope and helpful insight to other families, friends and co-workers of AS people. Many see Asperger Syndrome as another disability to put up with. However, as each person is valued and appreciated as an individual, relationships are much more meaningful. Solid, loving relationships are core to a great family and rich life. May God use this book to help bring joy and richness to you and your loved ones.

9101066